THE UK AIR FRYER COOI... WITH COLOURED PICTURES

Lots of easy and delicious recipes to prepare quickly, using traditional English ingredients and European measurements.

Mandy J. Smithson

AIR FRYER: WHAT IS IT?

Air Fryer is an appliance that typically has an egg-shaped, more or less square shape, with an extractable basket on which the dishes to be cooked are placed. It uses the concept of cooking with high temperatures up to 200° allowing a very healthy "frying-not-frying" of fresh and frozen foods. So forget the idea of a fryer where the dishes are immersed in abundant oil, because the amount of oil used in the air fryer is a few teaspoons or some "puffs" from a nebulizer. Real frying in abundant boiling oil is as good as "dangerous" especially if abused or not the necessary precautions are not taken. In the air fryer, the oil never reaches the smoking point and therefore is not toxic as it could be for frying. Hot air, which reaches high temperatures, circulates in the air fryer chamber allowing the dishes to be cooked uniformly both externally and internally. This way you can cook meat, fish, vegetables and a thousand other dishes in a few minutes: in short, you can make lots of recipes with the air fryer. Meat cooked in air fryer is juicy, tender and soft, excess fat drains to the bottom and does not remain inside the meat giving an exceptional taste.

HOW DOES AN AIR FRYER WORK? USE AND MAINTENANCE

An air fryer works by using a special cooking chamber. Before analysing how it works, it is important to understand a fundamental concept: fried food does not get its particular flavour and crispiness from the oil, but from the high temperatures the oil reaches. In an air fryer, oil is not necessary as it uses air as a heat carrier. The heated air is blasted into the cooking chamber at high speed, providing uniform and complete cooking of the food, with performance similar to that of a traditional fryer. In an air fryer, the food is completely surrounded by the heat carrier, and as a result, the food becomes crispy on the outside and tender on the inside. These small but functional appliances are able to reach very high cooking temperatures, around 200°C. This, of course, requires a rather high electricity consumption, with an absorption of between 800 and 2000 watts. However, the higher consumption is offset by the faster heating and cooking speed of the appliance, with much shorter times than a traditional oven; the savings on the purchase of oil for frying; and, last but not least, a healthier kitchen. The maintenance and cleaning of the air fryer is also extremely simple: the body of the machine should be cleaned with a damp cloth, while the basket where the food will be placed can be conveniently washed in the dishwasher, saving time and money.

THE DIFFERENCE BETWEEN A CLASSIC FRY-UP AND AN AIR FRYER

We all know and love the classic fry-up where we use a tool that is present in almost every Italian household: the oil fryer. Basically, it is an appliance equipped with a basket that needs to be filled with oil, which, when heated, takes care of cooking the food. The results are undoubtedly tasty, but this taste comes at a price: the traditional fried food is not at all healthy. Fried foods are very fatty and, in an age like ours, dominated by sedentariness, they can be the doorway to many health problems, above all obesity. However, technology seems to have found a remedy for this problem thanks to the development of the air fryer, a small appliance that combines the taste given to the dishes by the traditional fryer with the benefits of cooking in a traditional ventilated oven, with reduced use of oil and, consequently, greater healthiness of the dishes.

THE ADVANTAGES OF AN AIR FRYER

An air fryer is a very versatile appliance, contrary to what is thought: it replaces pans, ovens and of course the classic oil fryer, for a healthy kitchen that suits the tastes of all family members. Among the first features of this small gadget we can cite, first of all, the reduced or non-existent use of oil; indeed, it is sufficient to add a teaspoon, where required, otherwise it is possible to cook without any added fats. An ensuing advantage, not to be underestimated, is the absence of bad odours. The air fryer can be compared to a small electric oven, with the difference that, in the first case, there is an air circulation system which makes the dishes crispy and dry. Let's sum up and take a look at the advantages of this precious home appliance: -fried with less fat, lighter and healthier; -possibility to consume fried foods occasionally even for those with cholesterol problems, without feeling guilty; -possibility to make many different preparations, sweet and savoury; -less dirty cooking and no bad odours; -using minimal amounts of oil, which, among other things, not reaching the smoking point, does not risk becoming toxic; -easy and quick cleaning of the machine; -cooking without risks: you will no longer have to deal with oil splashes and hot pans; -significant gain in terms of economics and health.

WHICH MODEL TO CHOOSE?

There are numerous models of air fryers on the market, of course, depending on the model used and the power it is able to generate, you will have a different yield, in terms of the amount of food that can be cooked, and efficiency, from an energy consumption point of view; so it is important to choose the air fryer most suitable for our needs, evaluating different aspects, such as the number of components to be cooked for, the type of cooking we want to achieve, the space available in our kitchen. Other reference parameters to be taken into consideration when buying an air fryer, based on our needs, are: -Basket capacity, which can range from 1-3 liters for two people to 9 liters for cooking for more than eight people. -Maximum temperature (maximum 200 degrees). -Adjustable temperature, which guarantees the right level of crispness for each food. -Presence of a timer, thanks to which, through a particular sound, the fryer warns when it has finished cooking; some more sophisticated ones also sound when it is time to turn or move the food. -Heating times, so that it is possible to save on consumption where the reaching of the chosen temperature does not exceed three minutes. -Display with preset programs, thanks to which we just need a click to start the cooking most suitable for the dish we want to prepare, without having to worry about setting times and degrees.

BREAKFAST

Air Fryer Bacon

Preparation time: 10 minutes
Cooking time: 10 minutes
Number of servings: 4

Ingredients:
- 8 bacon pieces
- Salt and pepper, to taste

Directions:
1. Preheat the air fryer to 200°C.
2. Add the slices of bacon to the air fryer and spritz with cooking oil.
3. Sprinkle with salt and pepper, to taste.
4. Cook the bacon for 10 minutes, flipping it halfway through.
5. Serve hot.

Nutritional values: Calories: 157kcal, Carbohydrates: 0g, Protein: 8.7g, Fat: 13.9g, Cholesterol: 36mg.

Air Fryer French Toast

Preparation time: 10 minutes
Cooking time: 10 minutes
Number of servings: 4

Ingredients:
- 4 slices of white bread
- 2 eggs
- 2 tablespoons of milk
- 1 teaspoon of ground cinnamon
- 1 tablespoon of brown sugar
- 1/4 teaspoon of vanilla extract
- Pinch of salt

Directions:
1. In a bowl, stir together the eggs, milk, cinnamon, brown sugar, vanilla, and salt.
2. Dip each slice of bread into the egg mixture, coating both sides.
3. Place the coated slices of bread into the air fryer.
4. Cook for 10 minutes, flipping the slices halfway through.
5. Serve hot with maple syrup.

Nutritional values: Calories: 218kcal, Carbohydrates: 22.2g, Protein: 9.6g, Fat: 10.1g, Cholesterol: 134mg.

Air Fryer Sausage and Egg Muffins

Preparation time: 10 minutes
Cooking time: 15 minutes
Number of servings: 4

Ingredients:
- 4 large eggs

- 4 breakfast sausages
- 80g of shredded cheese
- Salt and pepper, to taste

Directions:
1. Preheat the air fryer to 180°C.
2. Grease 4 sections of a muffin tin with cooking oil.
3. Place a sausage in each section of the muffin tin.
4. Crack an egg into each section of the muffin tin, over the sausage.
5. Sprinkle the shredded cheese and season with salt and pepper, to taste.
6. Cook the muffins in the air fryer for 15 minutes.
7. Serve hot.

Nutritional values: Calories: 248kcal, Carbohydrates: 0.7g, Protein: 12.6g, Fat: 20.2g, Cholesterol: 195mg.

Air Fryer Hash Browns

Preparation time: 10 minutes
Cooking time: 10 minutes
Number of servings: 4

Ingredients:
- 1 large potato, peeled and grated
- 2 tablespoons of olive oil
- Salt and pepper, to taste

Directions:
1. Start by setting the air fryer to 200°C.
2. Place the grated potatoes in a bowl and season with salt and pepper, to taste.
3. Drizzle the olive oil over the potatoes and mix to combine.
4. After adding the potatoes to the air fryer, cook them for 10 minutes, turning them over halfway.
5. Serve hot.

Nutritional values: Calories: 123kcal, Carbohydrates: 17g, Protein: 2.2g, Fat: 5.5g, Cholesterol: 0mg.

Air Fryer Pop Tarts

Preparation time: 10 minutes
Cooking time: 12 minutes
Number of servings: 4

Ingredients:
- 4 pieces of ready-made puff pastry
- 2 tablespoons of strawberry jam
- 2 tablespoons of icing sugar
- 2 tablespoons of melted butter

Directions:
1. Preheat the air fryer to 180°C.
2. Cut the puff pastry into 8 equal rectangles.
3. Spread the strawberry jam on 4 of the rectangles.
4. Place the other 4 rectangles on top to form a tart. Press the edges together to seal them.
5. Place the tarts in the air fryer and fry for 12 minutes.
6. Take the tarts out of the air fryer and brush with melted butter.
7. Sprinkle with icing sugar and serve immediately.

Nutritional values: Calories: 290, Fat: 17 g, Carbohydrates: 25 g, Protein: 4 g, Fiber: 2 g, Sugar: 5 g

Air Fryer Baked Beans

Preparation time: 5 minutes
Cooking time: 15 minutes
Number of servings: 4

Ingredients:
- 2 cans of baked beans
- 2 tablespoons of tomato puree
- 2 tablespoons of brown sugar
- 1 teaspoon of Worcestershire sauce

Directions:
1. Start by setting the air fryer to 200°C.
2. Pour the cans of beans into a bowl.
3. Add the tomato puree, brown sugar, and Worcestershire sauce.
4. Stir together until all ingredients are combined.
5. Place the mixture in the air fryer and fry for 15 minutes.
6. Take the beans out of the air fryer and serve.

Nutritional values: Calories: 200, Fat: 0 g, Carbohydrates: 36 g, Protein: 11 g, Fiber: 5 g, Sugar: 17 g

Air Fryer Fried Eggs

Preparation time: 5 minutes
Cooking time: 5 minutes
Number of servings: 4

Ingredients:
- 4 eggs
- 2 tablespoons of vegetable oil
- Salt and pepper to taste

Directions:

1. Preheat the air fryer to 180°C.
2. Grease the air fryer basket with the vegetable oil.
3. Crack the eggs into the basket and season with salt and pepper.
4. Place the basket in the air fryer and fry for 5 minutes.
5. Remove the fried eggs from the air fryer and serve them.

Nutritional values: Calories: 90, Fat: 7 g, Carbohydrates: 0 g, Protein: 6 g, Fiber: 0 g, Sugar: 0 g

Air Fryer Yorkshire Puddings

Preparation time: 10 minutes
Cooking time: 15 minutes
Number of servings: 4

Ingredients:
- 250 g of plain flour
- 2 eggs
- 250 ml of milk
- 2 tablespoons of vegetable oil
- Salt and pepper to taste

Directions:
1. Preheat the air fryer to 200°C.
2. Grease the air fryer basket with the vegetable oil.
3. In a bowl, mix together the flour, eggs, milk, salt and pepper.
4. Pour the batter into the basket and place in the air fryer.
5. Fry for 15 minutes.
6. Take the Yorkshire puddings out of the air fryer and serve.

Nutritional values: Calories: 180, Fat: 10 g, Carbohydrates: 15 g, Protein: 6 g, Fiber: 0 g, Sugar: 1 g

Air fryer Pancakes

Preparation time: 10 minutes
Cooking time: 10 minutes
Number of servings: 4

Ingredients:
- 500 g of all-purpose flour
- 2 teaspoons of baking powder
- 1 teaspoon of baking soda
- 1 teaspoon of salt
- 2 tablespoons of sugar
- 2 eggs
- 500 ml of buttermilk
- 2 tablespoons of melted butter

Directions:
1. Combine the flour, baking powder, baking soda, salt, and sugar in a large bowl.
2. In a separate bowl, whisk together the eggs, buttermilk and melted butter.
3. Add the wet ingredients to the dry ingredients and stir until everything is just blended together. Do not over mix.
4. Preheat your air fryer to 180° C.
5. Grease the air fryer basket with cooking spray.
6. Drop spoonfuls of the pancake batter into the air fryer basket.
7. Cook the pancakes for 5 minutes, then flip them over and cook for an additional 5 minutes.
8. Serve the pancakes hot with your favorite toppings.

Nutritional Values: Calories: 283, Carbs: 44 g, Protein: 8 g, Fat: 7 g, Saturated Fat: 3 g, Sodium: 593 mg, Sugar: 6 g

Air Fryer Scones

Preparation time: 10-15 minutes
Cooking time: 10-15 minutes
Number of servings: 4

Ingredients:
- 500 g of self-raising flour
- 4 tablespoons of chilled butter, cut into cubes
- 250 g of cold milk
- 2 tablespoons of sugar
- ½ teaspoon of salt

Directions:
1. Preheat the air fryer to 175°C.
2. In a bowl, mix together the flour, butter, milk, sugar, and salt.
3. Knead the dough until it comes together and is smooth.
4. Grease the air fryer basket with oil or non-stick cooking spray.
5. Roll the dough into a circle about 1cm thick and cut into 4 wedges.
6. Place the wedges in the air fryer basket.
7. Fry for 10 to 15 minutes, or until thoroughly cooked and golden brown.
8. Serve warm with your favorite toppings!

Nutritional values: Calories: 320, Fat: 12g, Carbohydrates: 44g, Protein: 7g

Air Fryer Cinnamon Rolls

Preparation time: 20-25 minutes
Cooking time: 15-20 minutes
Number of servings: 4

Ingredients:
- 500 g of all purpose flour
- 2 teaspoons of baking powder
- 3 tablespoons of sugar
- 1 teaspoon of salt
- 250 ml of milk
- 2 tablespoons of melted butter
- 2 tablespoons of cinnamon
- 100 g of brown sugar
- 2 tablespoons of melted butter

Directions:
1. In a bowl, whisk together the flour, baking powder, salt and sugar.
2. In a separate bowl, whisk together the milk and melted butter.
3. Pour the wet ingredients into the dry ingredients and mix until combined.
4. On a lightly floured surface, roll out the dough into a rectangle.
5. Spread the melted butter across the dough, then dust with cinnamon and brown sugar.
6. Roll the dough up into a log and cut into 4 rolls.
7. Preheat the air fryer to 180°C.
8. Grease the air fryer basket with oil or non-stick cooking spray.
9. Place the rolls in the air fryer basket and fry for 15-20 minutes, or until golden brown and cooked through.

10. Serve warm with your favorite toppings!

Nutritional values: Calories: 400, Fat: 16g, Carbohydrates: 57g, Protein: 7g

Air Fryer Cheese and Bacon Omelette

Preparation time: 5-10 minutes
Cooking time: 10-15 minutes
Number of servings: 2

Ingredients:
- 4 eggs
- 2 tablespoons of shredded cheese
- 4 strips of cooked bacon, crumbled
- 2 tablespoons of chopped chives
- Salt and pepper, to taste

Directions:
1. Turn the air fryer on at 180°C.
2. Grease the air fryer basket with oil or non-stick cooking spray.
3. Combine the eggs, cheese, bacon, chives, salt, and pepper in a bowl.
4. Pour the egg mixture into the air fryer basket and spread evenly.
5. Fry for 10-15 minutes, or until golden brown and cooked through.
6. Serve warm with your favorite toppings!

Nutritional values: Calories: 260, Fat: 19g, Carbohydrates: 2g, Protein: 16g

Air Fryer Scotch Eggs

Preparation Time: 20 minutes
Cooking Time: 10-12 minutes
Number of Servings: 4

Ingredients:
- 4 hard-boiled eggs
- 200g sausage meat
- 100g plain flour
- 1 egg, beaten
- 1 teaspoon smoked paprika
- Salt and pepper, to taste

Directions:
1. Preheat the air fryer to 200°C.
2. Peel the hard-boiled eggs and set aside.
3. In a bowl, mix the sausage meat with the smoked paprika and season with salt and pepper.
4. Divide the sausage meat into four equal portions and shape each portion into a disc.
5. Place an egg in the centre of each disc and wrap the sausage meat around the egg, moulding it to shape.
6. Place the flour and beaten egg in separate shallow bowls.
7. Dip each Scotch egg in the flour, then the egg, and then back into the flour.
8. Place the Scotch eggs in the air fryer basket and cook for 10-12 minutes, or until golden and cooked through.

Nutritional Values: Calories: 233, Protein: 13.2g, Carbs: 5.1g, Fat: 17.2g

Air Fryer English Muffins

Preparation Time: 15 minutes
Cooking Time: 6-8 minutes
Number of Servings: 8

Ingredients:
- 8 English muffins
- 2 tablespoons butter, melted
- 2 teaspoons sugar

Directions:
1. Preheat the air fryer to 200°C.
2. Cut each English muffin in half and brush with the melted butter.
3. Sprinkle the sugar over the muffins.
4. Place the English muffins in the air fryer basket and cook for 6-8 minutes, or until golden and toasted.

Nutritional Values: Calories: 154, Protein: 3.8g, Carbs: 16.2g, Fat: 8.8g

Air Fryer Toad in the Hole

Preparation Time: 10 minutes
Cooking Time: 20 minutes
Number of Servings: 4

Ingredients:
- 200g sausages
- 1 tablespoon vegetable oil
- 2 eggs
- 150ml milk

- 100g plain flour
- 1 Pinch of salt

Directions:
1. Preheat the air fryer to 200°C.
2. Place the sausages in the air fryer basket and cook for 10 minutes.
3. In a bowl, whisk together the eggs, milk, flour and salt to make a batter.
4. Grease the air fryer basket with the oil.
5. Place the sausages in the batter and carefully transfer them to the air fryer basket.
6. Cook for 10 minutes, or until the batter is golden and cooked through.

Nutritional Values: Calories: 333, Protein: 12.5g, Carbs: 19.9g, Fat: 22.2g

Air Fryer Sausage Patties

Preparation Time: 10 minutes
Cooking Time: 10-12 minutes
Number of Servings: 8

Ingredients:
- 500g sausage mince
- 1 onion, finely chopped
- 2 cloves garlic, minced
- 1 teaspoon smoked paprika
- Salt and pepper, to taste

Directions:
1. Preheat the air fryer to 200°C.
2. In a bowl, mix together the sausage mince, onion, garlic, smoked paprika and season with salt and pepper.
3. Divide the mixture into eight equal portions and shape into patties.
4. Put the patties in the air fryer basket and fry them for 10 to 12 minutes, or until they are brown and well done.

Nutritional Values: Calories: 211, Protein: 14.3g, Carbs: 1.3g, Fat: 17.3g

Air Fryer Cornish Pasties

Preparation Time: 15 minutes
Cooking Time: 15-20 minutes
Number of Servings: 6

Ingredients:
- 500g shortcrust pastry
- 350g potatoes, peeled and diced
- 1 onion, finely chopped
- 200g swede, peeled and diced
- 100g minced beef
- 1 teaspoon salt
- 1 teaspoon pepper
- 2 tablespoons butter, melted

Directions:
1. Preheat the air fryer to 180°C.
2. Combine the potatoes, onion, swede, minced meat, salt, and pepper in a bowl.
3. Cut the pastry into 6 equal circles and place 2 tablespoons of the mixture in the centre of each circle.
4. Fold the pastry over the filling and seal the edges with a fork.
5. Brush each pasty with melted butter.
6. Place the pasties in the air fryer basket and cook for 15-20 minutes, or until golden brown.
7. Serve hot.

Nutritional Values: Calories: 310, Carbohydrates: 27.6g, Protein: 11.2g, Fat: 16.5g, Saturated Fat: 7.5g, Fibre: 2.8g

Air Fryer Toads in Blankets

Preparation Time: 10 minutes
Cooking Time: 10 minutes
Number of Servings: 8

Ingredients:
- 8 Frankfurters (sausages)
- 8 slices of streaky bacon

Directions:
1. Start by setting the air fryer to 200°C.
2. Place a piece of bacon around each hot dog.
3. Place the wrapped frankfurters in the air fryer basket and cook for 10 minutes, or until the bacon is crispy.
4. Serve hot.

Nutritional Values: Calories: 284, Carbohydrates: 0.1g, Protein: 15.3g, Fat: 24.1g

Air Fryer Mini Quiches

Preparation Time: 10 minutes
Cooking Time: 15 minutes
Number of Servings: 6

Ingredients:
- 230g ready-made shortcrust pastry
- 2 eggs, beaten
- 150ml double cream
- 120g cheddar cheese, grated
- 2 tablespoons chopped chives
- Salt and pepper, to taste

Directions:
1. Preheat the air fryer to 180°C.
2. Cut the pastry into 6 circles and line the holes of a greased muffin tin.
3. In a bowl, mix together the eggs, cream, cheese, chives, and salt and pepper.
4. Divide the mixture between the pastry cases.
5. Place in the air fryer and cook for 15 minutes, or until golden brown.
6. Serve hot.

Nutritional Values: Calories: 289, Carbohydrates: 12.7g, Protein: 9.8g, Fat: 21.5g

Air Fryer Chorizo and Egg Muffins

Preparation Time: 10 minutes
Cooking Time: 15 minutes
Number of Servings: 12

Ingredients:
- 12 eggs
- 2 tablespoons olive oil
- 250g chorizo, diced
- 2 tablespoons chopped flat-leaf parsley
- Salt and pepper, to taste

Directions:
1. Preheat the air fryer to 180°C.
2. Grease 12 muffin holes.
3. In a bowl, whisk together the eggs, olive oil, chorizo, parsley, and salt and pepper.
4. Distribute the mixture among the muffin cavities.
5. Place in the air fryer and cook for 15 minutes, or until golden brown.
6. Serve hot.

Nutritional Values: Calories: 140, Carbohydrates: 1.2g, Protein: 9.3g

POULTRY AND TURKEY RECIPES

Air Fryer Chicken Breast

Preparation time: 10 minutes
Cooking time: 25 minutes
Number of servings: 4

Ingredients:
- 4 boneless, skinless chicken breasts
- 2 tablespoons olive oil
- 1 teaspoon garlic powder
- 1 teaspoon dried oregano
- 1 teaspoon paprika
- ½ teaspoon ground black pepper
- ½ teaspoon salt

Directions:
1. Start by setting the air fryer to 200°C.

2. Place the chicken breasts in a shallow dish and drizzle with olive oil.
3. In a small bowl, mix together the garlic powder, oregano, paprika, black pepper and salt.
4. Sprinkle the chicken breasts with the spice mixture.
5. Place the chicken breasts in the air fryer basket and cook for 20-25 minutes, flipping the chicken halfway through.
6. Remove from the air fryer and let rest for 5 minutes before serving.
Nutritional values: Calories: 165, Fat: 7 g, Carbohydrates: 0 g, Protein: 25 g

Air Fryer Chicken Wings

Preparation time: 10 minutes
Cooking time: 25 minutes
Number of servings: 4

Ingredients:
- 1kg chicken wings
- 2 tablespoons olive oil
- 2 teaspoons garlic powder
- 2 teaspoons dried oregano
- 2 teaspoons smoked paprika
- 1 teaspoon ground black pepper
- 1 teaspoon sea salt

Directions:
1. Preheat the air fryer to 200°C.
2. Place the chicken wings in a shallow dish and drizzle with olive oil.
3. In a small bowl, mix together the garlic powder, oregano, paprika, black pepper and salt.
4. Rub the spice mixture over the chicken wings.
5. Place the chicken wings in the air fryer basket and cook for 20-25 minutes, flipping the chicken halfway through.
6. Remove from the air fryer and let rest for 5 minutes before serving.

Nutritional values: Calories: 568, Fat: 45 g, Carbohydrates: 0 g, Protein: 32 g

Air Fryer Roast Chicken

Preparation time: 10 minutes
Cooking time: 40 minutes
Number of servings: 6

Ingredients:
- 1 whole chicken, about 1.5kg
- 2 tablespoons olive oil
- 2 teaspoons garlic powder
- 2 teaspoons dried oregano
- 2 teaspoons smoked paprika
- 1 teaspoon ground black pepper
- 1 teaspoon sea salt

Directions:
1. Start by setting the air fryer to 200°C.
2. Place the chicken in a shallow dish and drizzle with olive oil.
3. Combine the garlic powder, oregano, paprika, salt, black pepper, and in a small bowl.
4. Rub the spice mixture over the chicken.
5. Place the chicken in the air fryer basket and cook for 35-40 minutes, flipping the chicken halfway through.
6. Remove from the air fryer and let rest for 5 minutes before serving.

Nutritional values: Calories: 706, Fat: 37 g, Carbohydrates: 0 g, Protein: 84 g

Fryer Chicken Tenders

Preparation time: 10 minutes
Cooking time: 15 minutes
Number of servings: 4

Ingredients:
- 500g of chicken tenders
- 2 tablespoons olive oil
- 2 teaspoons garlic powder
- 2 teaspoons dried oregano
- 2 teaspoons smoked paprika
- 1 teaspoon ground black pepper
- 1 teaspoon sea salt

Directions:
1. Preheat the air fryer to 200°C.
2. Place the chicken tenders in a shallow dish and drizzle with olive oil.
3. In a small bowl, mix together the garlic powder, oregano, paprika, black pepper and salt.
4. Rub the spice mixture over the chicken tenders.
5. Place the chicken tenders in the air fryer basket and cook for 10-15 minutes, flipping the chicken halfway through.
6. Remove from the air fryer and let rest for 5 minutes before serving.

Nutritional values: Calories: 332, Fat: 16 g, Carbohydrates: 0 g, Protein: 41 g

Air Fryer Popcorn Chicken

Preparation time: 10 minutes
Cooking time: 15 minutes
Number of servings: 4

Ingredients:

- 500g chicken breast, cut into bite-sized pieces
- 2 tablespoons olive oil
- 2 teaspoons paprika
- 1 teaspoon garlic powder
- 2 tablespoons cornflour
- 1 teaspoon mustard powder
- 1 teaspoon dried oregano
- Salt and pepper, to taste

Directions:
1. Start by setting the air fryer to 200°C.
2. In a large bowl, combine the chicken pieces, olive oil, paprika, garlic powder, cornflour, mustard powder, oregano, salt and pepper.
3. Toss the chicken until evenly coated.
4. Place the chicken pieces in the air fryer and cook for 15 minutes, shaking the basket halfway through.
5. Serve with your favourite dipping sauce.

Nutritional Values: Calories: 320 kcal, Fat: 11.2 g, Carbohydrates: 7.1 g, Protein: 43.9 g

Air Fryer Chicken Kebabs

Preparation time: 15 minutes
Cooking time: 10 minutes
Number of servings: 4

Ingredients:
- 500g boneless skinless chicken breast, cubed
- 2 tablespoons olive oil
- 2 tablespoons honey
- 2 tablespoons soy sauce
- 1 teaspoon garlic powder
- 1 teaspoon smoked paprika
- 1 teaspoon dried oregano
- Salt and pepper, to taste

Directions:
1. Preheat the air fryer to 200°C.

2. In a large bowl, combine the chicken cubes, olive oil, honey, soy sauce, garlic powder, smoked paprika, oregano, salt and pepper.
3. Toss the chicken until evenly coated.
4. Thread the chicken cubes onto skewers and place in the air fryer.
5. Cook for 10 minutes, flipping the skewers halfway through.
6. Serve with your favourite dipping sauce.

Nutritional Values: Calories: 286, Fat: 8.3g, Carbohydrates: 13.3g, Protein: 37.3g

Air Fryer Chicken Nuggets

Preparation time: 10 minutes
Cooking time: 10 minutes
Number of servings: 4

Ingredients:
- 500g boneless skinless chicken breast, cubed
- 2 tablespoons olive oil
- 2 tablespoons all-purpose flour
- 1 teaspoon garlic powder
- 1 teaspoon paprika
- 1 teaspoon dried oregano
- Salt and pepper, to taste

Directions:
1. Preheat the air fryer to 200°C.

2. Combine the chicken cubes, olive oil, flour, garlic powder, paprika, oregano, salt, and pepper in a large mixing basin.
3. Toss the chicken until evenly coated.
4. Place the chicken cubes in the air fryer and cook for 10 minutes, shaking the basket every 2 minutes.
5. Toss with your favorite dipping sauce and serve.

Nutritional Values: Calories: 319 kcal, Fat: 13.2 g, Carbohydrates: 10.2 g, Protein: 41.3 g

Chicken Quesadillas

Preparation time: 10 minutes
Cooking time: 10 minutes
Number of servings: 4

Ingredients:
- 4 large flour tortillas
- 500g boneless skinless chicken breast, cooked and shredded
- 250g shredded Mexican cheese blend
- 120g salsa
- 2 tablespoons olive oil
- 1 teaspoon chilli powder
- 1 teaspoon garlic powder
- 1 teaspoon smoked paprika
- 1 teaspoon dried oregano
- Salt and pepper, to taste

Directions:
1. Preheat the air fryer to 200°C.
2. Place a tortilla on a flat surface.
3. Spread with 70g of cheese, 100g of the chicken, and 2 tablespoons of the salsa.
4. Top with another tortilla.
5. Brush the top of the tortilla with the olive oil.
6. Place in the air fryer and cook for 5 minutes, flipping halfway through.
7. Slice into wedges and serve with your favourite dipping sauce.

Nutritional Values: Calories: 431 kcal, Fat: 16.8 g, Carbohydrates: 36.7 g, Protein: 31.2 g

Air Fryer Chicken Fajitas

Preparation Time: 15 minutes
Cooking Time: 15 minutes
Number of Servings: 4

Ingredients:
- 1 large red bell pepper, cut into thin strips
- 1 large yellow bell pepper, cut into thin strips
- 1 large green bell pepper, cut into thin strips
- 2 cloves garlic, minced
- 2 tablespoons olive oil
- 1 teaspoon chili powder
- 1 teaspoon ground cumin
- 1 teaspoon paprika
- 500g chicken breast, cut into thin strips
- 2 limes, cut into wedges
- 4 soft flour tortillas
- Salt and pepper, to taste

Directions:
1. Preheat the air fryer to 200°C.
2. In a large bowl, combine the bell peppers, garlic, olive oil, chili powder, cumin, and paprika. Mix until the peppers are evenly coated.

3. Place the pepper mixture in the preheated air fryer and cook for 8 minutes.
4. Add the chicken to the air fryer and cook for an additional 6 minutes, or until the chicken is cooked through.
5. Remove the chicken and pepper mixture from the air fryer and serve on warm tortillas with lime wedges.
6. Season with salt and pepper, to taste.

Nutritional Values: Calories: 396 kcal, Fat: 11.7 g, Carbohydrates: 36.6 g, Protein: 33.2 g

Air Fryer Buffalo Wings

Preparation Time: 10 minutes
Cooking Time: 15 minutes
Number of Servings: 4

Ingredients:
- 500g chicken wings
- 4 tablespoons butter, melted
- 4 tablespoons hot sauce
- 2 tablespoons Worcestershire sauce
- 1 teaspoon garlic powder
- 1 teaspoon paprika
- Salt and pepper, to taste

Directions:
1. Preheat the air fryer to 200°C.
2. In a large bowl, combine the melted butter, hot sauce, Worcestershire sauce, garlic powder, and paprika. Mix until the ingredients are evenly combined.
3. Add the chicken wings to the bowl and toss to coat.
4. Place the chicken wings in the preheated air fryer and cook for 15 minutes, or until the chicken is cooked through.
5. Remove the chicken wings from the air fryer and serve.
6. Season with salt and pepper, to taste.

Nutritional Values: Calories: 541 kcal, Fat: 32.2 g, Carbohydrates: 5.9 g, Protein: 47.2 g

Air Fryer Chicken Fries

Preparation Time: 10 minutes
Cooking Time: 15 minutes
Number of Servings: 4

Ingredients:
- 1kg boneless, skinless chicken breasts, cut into strips
- 2 eggs, beaten
- 400g panko breadcrumbs
- 1 teaspoon garlic powder
- 1 teaspoon smoked paprika
- 1 teaspoon onion powder
- Salt and pepper, to taste

Directions:
1. Preheat the air fryer to 200°C.
2. Dip the chicken strips in the beaten eggs, then coat with the panko breadcrumbs.
3. Place the chicken strips in the preheated air fryer and cook for 15 minutes, or until the chicken is cooked through.
4. Remove the chicken fries from the air fryer and serve.
5. Sprinkle with garlic powder, smoked paprika, and onion powder.
6. Season with salt and pepper, to taste.

Nutritional Values: Calories: 790 kcal, Fat: 28.3 g, Carbohydrates: 76.2 g, Protein: 48.6 g

Air fryer chicken parmesan

Preparation time: 15 minutes
Cooking time: 15 minutes
Number of servings: 4

Ingredients:
- 4 boneless, skinless chicken breasts
- 40g plain flour
- 2 eggs
- 200g breadcrumbs
- 2 tablespoons of Italian herbs
- 2 tablespoons of garlic powder
- 2 tablespoons of olive oil
- 250g of grated mozzarella
- 250g of tomato sauce
- Salt and pepper, to taste

Directions:
1. Preheat the air fryer to 200C.
2. Cut the chicken breasts into thin strips and season with salt and pepper.
3. Place the flour in a bowl.
4. Beat the eggs in another bowl.
5. In a third bowl, mix the breadcrumbs, Italian herbs, and garlic powder.
6. Dip each chicken strip in the flour, then in the egg, and finally in the breadcrumb mixture.
7. Place the chicken strips in the air fryer and cook for 10 minutes or until golden brown.
8. Remove from the air fryer and top with mozzarella and tomato sauce.
9. Cook for a further 5 minutes or until the cheese is melted and bubbling.
10. Serve the chicken parmesan with a side salad.

Nutritional values: Calories: 575, Fat: 24g, Carbohydrates: 39g, Protein: 43g

Air Fryer Baked Chicken

Preparation time: 10 minutes
Cooking time: 40 minutes
Number of servings: 4

Ingredients:
- 4 chicken breasts (400 g)
- 1 teaspoon of paprika
- 1 teaspoon of garlic powder
- 1 teaspoon of onion powder
- 2 tablespoons of olive oil
- Salt and pepper, to taste

Directions:
1. Preheat the air fryer to 180°C.
2. In a large bowl, combine the paprika, garlic powder, onion powder, olive oil, salt and pepper.
3. Add the chicken breasts to the bowl and mix until they are evenly coated.
4. Place the chicken breasts in the air fryer basket.
5. Cook for 40 minutes, flipping the chicken halfway through.
6. Serve hot.

Nutritional values: Calories: 170, Fat: 7 g, Carbohydrates: 1 g, Protein: 24 g

Air fryer crispy chicken

Preparation Time: 10 minutes
Cooking Time: 12 minutes
Number of Servings: 4

Ingredients:
* 1.5 kg of chicken wings
* 2 tablespoons of olive oil
* 2 tablespoons of freshly chopped herbs (rosemary, thyme, oregano)
* 1 teaspoon of garlic powder
* 1 teaspoon of onion powder
* 1 teaspoon of paprika
* Salt and pepper to taste

Directions:
1. Preheat your air fryer to 180°C.
2. In a large bowl, mix together the olive oil, herbs, garlic powder, onion powder, paprika, salt and pepper.
3. Add the chicken wings to the bowl and toss to coat.
4. Place the chicken wings in the air fryer basket, making sure not to overcrowd.
5. Cook for 12 minutes or until the chicken wings are golden and crispy.
6. Serve immediately with your favorite sides. Enjoy!

Nutritional Values: Calories: 390 kcal, Fat: 20g, Carbohydrates: 0g, Protein: 45g

Air fryer fried chicken

Preparation time: 20 minutes

Cooking time: 15 minutes
Number of servings: 4

Ingredients:
* 1.2 kg of chicken breasts, cut into pieces
* 2 tablespoons of olive oil
* 2 teaspoons of garlic powder
* 1 teaspoon of oregano
* 1 teaspoon of paprika
* 1 teaspoon of black pepper
* 1 teaspoon of salt

Directions:
1. Preheat air fryer to 180°C.
2. In a large bowl, combine chicken, olive oil, garlic powder, oregano, paprika, black pepper and salt. Mix until chicken is well coated.
3. Place chicken pieces in the air fryer basket, ensuring that pieces don't overlap.
4. Cook for 15 minutes, flipping chicken pieces over halfway through cooking time.
5. Remove chicken from air fryer and serve.

Nutritional values: Calories: 153, Carbohydrates: 0g, Fats: 8g, Protein: 17g

Air fryer chicken and waffles

Preparation Times: 15 minutes
Cooking Times: 15 minutes
Number of Servings: 4

Ingredients:
* 2 boneless, skinless chicken breasts, cut into strips
* Salt and pepper to taste
* 120g of all-purpose flour
* 2 large eggs, beaten
* 220g of panko breadcrumbs
* 1 teaspoon garlic powder
* 2 tablespoons (30 ml) vegetable oil
* 4 waffles, cooked according to package instructions

Directions:
1. Preheat your air fryer to 180°C.
2. Season the chicken strips with salt and pepper.
3. Place the flour, eggs, panko breadcrumbs, garlic powder, and oil in separate shallow dishes.
4. Dip each chicken strip in the flour, then the egg, then the breadcrumbs, and place in the air fryer basket.
5. Cook the chicken strips for 10 minutes, flipping them halfway through.
6. Serve the chicken strips on top of the waffles and enjoy.

Nutritional Values: Calories: 537 kcal, Carbohydrates: 46.9 g, Protein: 28.5 g, Fat: 24.4 g

- 2 tablespoons lemon juice
- Salt, to taste

Directions:
1. Preheat your air fryer to 180°C.
2. In a bowl, mix together the oil, garlic, ginger, tandoori masala, garam masala, chili powder, yoghurt and lemon juice.
3. Rub the marinade over the chicken thighs, making sure they are completely coated.
4. Place the chicken thighs in the air fryer basket and cook for 15 minutes or until the chicken is cooked through.
5. Sprinkle with salt, to taste.
6. Serve with your favorite side dish.

Nutritional Values: Calories: 300, Fat: 16g, Carbohydrates: 6g, Protein: 33g

Air fryer chicken tandoori

Preparation Time: 10 minutes
Cooking Time: 15 minutes
Number of Servings: 4

Ingredients:
- 1 kg chicken thighs
- 2 tablespoons vegetable oil
- 2 teaspoons garlic, minced
- 2 teaspoons ginger, minced
- 2 tablespoons tandoori masala
- 1 tablespoon garam masala
- 1 teaspoon chili powder
- 2 tablespoons yoghurt

Air fryer chicken tikka masala

Preparation time: 15 minutes
Cooking time: 30 minutes
Number of servings: 4

Ingredients:
- 500g chicken thigh fillets, cubed
- 1 onion, diced
- 2 cloves garlic, minced
- 1 tablespoon grated ginger
- 1 teaspoon ground cumin
- 1 teaspoon garam masala
- 1 teaspoon ground coriander
- 1 teaspoon ground turmeric
- 1/2 teaspoon chilli powder
- 1/4 teaspoon ground cardamom
- 2 tablespoons tomato paste
- 250ml plain yoghurt
- 2 tablespoons vegetable oil
- 2 tablespoons chopped fresh coriander

Directions:

1. In a large bowl, mix together the cubed chicken, onion, garlic, ginger, cumin, garam masala, coriander, turmeric, chilli powder, and cardamom.
Add the tomato paste and yoghurt and mix until everything is evenly blended.
2. Preheat the air fryer to 200°C.
3. Grease the air fryer basket with the vegetable oil.
4. Place the chicken mixture into the air fryer basket and cook for 15 minutes.
5. After 15 minutes, flip the chicken and cook for a further 15 minutes.
6. Once cooked, serve the chicken tikka masala with fresh coriander and sides of your choice.

Nutritional Values: Calories: 330, Fat: 20 g, Carbohydrates: 10 g, Protein: 30 g, Sodium: 300 mg

- 1 teaspoon of salt
- ½ teaspoon of black pepper
- 2 tablespoons of olive oil

Directions:
1. Preheat the air fryer to 200°C.
2. In a bowl, combine the garlic, smoked paprika, garlic powder, onion powder, oregano, chili powder, salt and pepper.
3. Rub the chicken thighs with the olive oil and the seasoning mix.
4. Put the chicken thighs in the air fryer basket and cook for 20 minutes, turning the chicken halfway through the baking period.
5. Once cooked, remove from the air fryer and serve.

Nutritional Values: Calories: 230, Fat: 14 g, Carbohydrates: 0 g, Protein: 23 g, Sodium: 360 mg, Cholesterol: 70 mg

Air Fryer Spicy Chicken Thighs

Preparation time: 10 minutes
Cooking time: 20 minutes
Number of servings: 4

Ingredients:
- 4 chicken thighs
- 4 cloves of garlic, minced
- 1 teaspoon of smoked paprika
- 1 teaspoon of garlic powder
- 1 teaspoon of onion powder
- 1 teaspoon of dried oregano
- 1 teaspoon of chili powder

Air Fryer Chicken Caesar Salad

Preparation Time: 10 minutes
Cooking Time: 15 minutes
Number of Servings: 2

Ingredients:
- Chicken breasts: 400g
- Olive oil: 2 tablespoons
- Salt and pepper: to taste
- Caesar salad dressing: 6 tablespoons
- Romaine lettuce: 1 head
- Parmesan cheese: 50g
- Croutons: 60g

Directions:
1. Preheat the air fryer to 200°C.
2. Rub the chicken breasts with olive oil, salt and pepper. Place them in the air fryer basket.
3. Cook the chicken breasts in the air fryer for 10 minutes, flipping once halfway through.

4. Remove the chicken and let it rest for 5 minutes. Then slice the chicken into strips.

5. In a bowl, mix together the Caesar salad dressing and the sliced chicken.

6. Place the Romaine lettuce in a large bowl and top with the chicken Caesar salad dressing mixture.

7. Sprinkle the Parmesan cheese and croutons on top.

8. Serve the salad immediately.

Nutritional Values: Calories: 343, Fat: 16.8g, Carbohydrates: 15.3g, Protein: 29.3g

BEEF, PORK AND LAMB RECIPES

Air Fryer Beef Burgers

Preparation time: 10 minutes
Cooking time: 10 minutes
Number of servings: 4

Ingredients:
- 500g minced beef
- 2 cloves garlic, crushed
- 1 teaspoon dried oregano
- 1 teaspoon dried thyme
- 1 teaspoon smoked paprika
- 1 teaspoon ground cumin
- 1 teaspoon fine sea salt
- 1 teaspoon freshly ground black pepper

Directions:
1. In a medium bowl, combine all the ingredients and mix together until evenly combined.
2. Form into 4 equal sized patties.
3. Preheat your air fryer to 180°C.
4. Place the patties in the air fryer and cook for 10 minutes, flipping halfway through.
5. Serve with your favourite burger toppings.

Nutrition Information: Calories: 516, Carbohydrates: 8.7 g, Protein: 30.7 g, Fat: 37.7 g

Air Fryer Steak Fries

Preparation time: 10 minutes
Cooking time: 15 minutes
Number of servings: 4

Ingredients:
- 400g potatoes, cut into thick wedges
- 2 tablespoons olive oil
- 1 teaspoon garlic powder
- 1 teaspoon smoked paprika
- 1 teaspoon dried oregano
- 1 teaspoon fine sea salt

Directions:
1. Place the potatoes in a medium bowl and add the olive oil, garlic powder, smoked paprika, oregano and salt.
2. Toss to combine.
3. Preheat your air fryer to 200°C.
4. Place the potatoes in the air fryer and cook for 15 minutes, flipping halfway through.
5. Serve as a side dish.

Nutrition Information: Calories: 222, Carbohydrates: 30.3 g, Protein: 3.2 g, Fat: 10.3 g

Air Fryer Beef Roast

Preparation time: 10 minutes
Cooking time: 30 minutes
Number of servings: 6

Ingredients:
- 600g beef roast
- 2 tablespoons olive oil
- 2 cloves garlic, crushed
- 1 teaspoon dried oregano
- 1 teaspoon dried thyme
- 1 teaspoon smoked paprika
- 1 teaspoon ground cumin
- 1 teaspoon fine sea salt
- 1 teaspoon freshly ground black pepper

Directions:
1. Rub the beef roast with the olive oil, garlic, oregano, thyme, smoked paprika, cumin, salt and pepper.
2. Preheat your air fryer to 180°C.
3. Place the roast in the air fryer and cook for 30 minutes, flipping halfway through.
4. Allow the roast to sit for 10 minutes before cutting and presenting.

Nutrition Information: Calories: 322, Carbohydrates: 0.5 g, Protein: 44.2 g, Fat: 14.3 g

Bangers and Mash

Preparation time: 10 minutes
Cooking time: 20 minutes
Number of servings: 4

Ingredients:
- 400g potatoes, cut into thick wedges
- 2 tablespoons olive oil
- 1 teaspoon garlic powder
- 1 teaspoon smoked paprika
- 1 teaspoon dried oregano
- 1 teaspoon fine sea salt
- 400g sausages

Directions:
1. Place the potatoes in a medium bowl and add the olive oil, garlic powder, smoked paprika, oregano and salt.
2. Toss to combine.
3. Preheat your air fryer to 200°C.

4. Place the potatoes in the air fryer and cook for 15 minutes, flipping halfway through.
5. Add the sausages to the air fryer and cook for an additional 5 minutes.
6. Serve the sausages and potatoes with your favourite accompaniments.

Nutrition Information: Calories: 605, Carbohydrates: 50.3 g, Protein: 20.2 g, Fat: 37.2 g

Air Fryer Bacon Wrapped Beef Tenderloin

Preparation time: 10 minutes
Cooking time: 25 minutes
Number of Servings: 4

Ingredients:
- 800g Beef Tenderloin
- 8 slices of bacon
- 2 tablespoons olive oil
- 2 teaspoon garlic powder
- 2 teaspoon dried oregano
- 2 teaspoon salt
- 1 teaspoon black pepper

Directions:
1. Preheat the air fryer to 200°C.
2. Cut the beef tenderloin into 4 equal pieces.
3. Wrap each piece of beef with two slices of bacon.

4. In a small bowl, mix together the olive oil, garlic powder, oregano, salt, and pepper.
5. Brush the mixture over the bacon-wrapped beef tenderloins.
6. Place the bacon-wrapped beef tenderloins in the air fryer and cook for 25 minutes or until the bacon is crispy.
7. Serve with your favorite sides.

Nutritional Values: Calories: 403, Fat: 22.1g, Carbohydrates: 0.5g, Protein: 43.2g

Air Fryer Beef Kebabs

Preparation time: 10 minutes
Cooking time: 10 minutes
Number of Servings: 4

Ingredients:
- 500g sirloin steak, cubed
- 1 large red onion, cubed
- 2 bell peppers, cubed
- 2 tablespoons olive oil
- 2 teaspoons garlic powder
- 2 teaspoons smoked paprika
- 1 teaspoon salt
- 1 teaspoon black pepper

Directions:
1. Preheat the air fryer to 200°C.
2. In a medium bowl, combine the cubed steak, onion, and bell peppers.
3. In a small bowl, mix together the olive oil, garlic powder, smoked paprika, salt, and pepper.
4. Drizzle the mixture over the cubed steak and vegetables and mix until everything is evenly coated.
5. Thread the steak and vegetables onto 4 skewers.
6. Place the kebabs in the air fryer and cook for 10 minutes or until the steak is cooked to your desired doneness.
7. Serve with your favorite sides.

Nutritional Values: Calories: 351, Fat: 19.1g, Carbohydrates: 10.5g, Protein: 32.3g

Air Fryer Pulled Pork

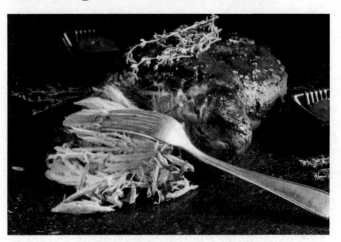

Preparation time: 10 minutes
Cooking time: 25 minutes
Number of Servings: 4

Ingredients:
- 800g pork shoulder
- 2 tablespoons olive oil
- 2 teaspoons garlic powder
- 2 teaspoons smoked paprika
- 1 teaspoon salt
- 1 teaspoon black pepper

Directions:
1. Preheat the air fryer to 200°C.
2. Place the pork shoulder in the air fryer and cook for 25 minutes or until the pork is cooked through.
3. Remove the pork from the air fryer and shred it using two forks.
4. In a small bowl, mix together the olive oil, garlic powder, smoked paprika, salt, and pepper.
5. Drizzle the mixture over the shredded pork and mix until everything is evenly coated.
6. Place the shredded pork back in the air fryer and cook for 5 minutes or until the pork is crispy.
7. Serve with your favorite sides.

Nutritional Values: Calories: 271, Fat: 16.3g, Carbohydrates: 1.9g, Protein: 26.4g

Air Fryer Bacon-Wrapped Pork Loin

Preparation time: 10 minutes
Cooking time: 25 minutes
Number of Servings: 4

Ingredients:
- 500g pork loin
- 8 slices of bacon
- 2 tablespoons olive oil
- 2 teaspoons garlic powder
- 2 teaspoons dried oregano
- 1 teaspoon salt
- 1 teaspoon black pepper

Directions:
1. Preheat the air fryer to 200°C.
2. Wrap the pork loin with the bacon slices.
3. In a small bowl, mix together the olive oil, garlic powder, oregano, salt, and pepper.
4. Brush the mixture over the bacon-wrapped pork loin.
5. Place the bacon-wrapped pork loin in the air fryer and cook for 25 minutes or until the bacon is crispy.
6. Serve with your favorite sides.

Nutritional Values: Calories: 431, Fat: 25.7g, Carbohydrates: 0.5g, Protein: 42.2g

Air Fryer Pork Chops

Preparation time: 10 minutes
Cooking time: 8 minutes
Number of servings: 4

Ingredients:
- 4 pork loin chops, about 150g each
- 1 tablespoon olive oil
- 1 teaspoon garlic powder
- 1 teaspoon paprika
- ½ teaspoon salt
- ½ teaspoon ground black pepper

Directions:
1. Preheat your air fryer to 180°C.
2. Rub the pork chops with olive oil, garlic powder, paprika, salt, and pepper.
3. Place the pork chops in the air fryer.
4. Cook for 8 minutes or until the pork chops reach an internal temperature of 75°C.
5. Serve immediately.

Nutritional values: Calories: 240; Total Fat: 10g; Saturated Fat: 3g; Cholesterol: 65mg; Sodium: 300mg; Carbohydrates: 1g; Protein: 33g.

Air Fryer Pork Tenderloin

Preparation time: 10 minutes
Cooking time: 10 minutes
Number of servings: 4

Ingredients:

- 2 pork tenderloins (1kg total)
- 2 tablespoons olive oil
- 2 teaspoons smoked paprika
- 1 teaspoon garlic powder
- 1 teaspoon dried oregano
- ½ teaspoon salt
- ½ teaspoon ground black pepper

Directions:
1. Preheat your air fryer to 190°C.
2. Rub the pork tenderloins with olive oil, smoked paprika, garlic powder, oregano, salt, and pepper.
3. Place the pork tenderloins in the air fryer.
4. Cook for 10 minutes and serve immediately.

Nutritional values: Calories: 360; Total Fat: 21g; Saturated Fat: 6g; Cholesterol: 95mg; Sodium: 520mg; Carbohydrates: 1g; Protein: 40g.

Air Fryer Barbecue Ribs

Preparation time: 10 minutes
Cooking time: 25 minutes
Number of servings: 4

Ingredients:
- 1kg pork ribs
- 2 tablespoons olive oil
- 2 tablespoons barbecue sauce
- 2 teaspoons smoked paprika
- 1 teaspoon garlic powder
- 1 teaspoon dried oregano

- ½ teaspoon salt
- ½ teaspoon ground black pepper

Directions:
1. Preheat your air fryer to 190°C.
2. Rub the pork ribs with olive oil, barbecue sauce, smoked paprika, garlic powder, oregano, salt, and pepper.
3. Place the pork ribs in the air fryer.
4. Cook for 25 minutes or until the pork ribs reach an internal temperature of 75°C.
5. Serve immediately.

Nutritional values: Calories: 515; Total Fat: 36g; Saturated Fat: 11g; Cholesterol: 95mg; Sodium: 880mg; Carbohydrates: 3g; Protein: 44g.

Air Fryer Sticky Pork Ribs

Preparation time: 10 minutes
Cooking time: 25 minutes
Number of servings: 4

Ingredients:
- 1kg pork ribs
- 2 tablespoons olive oil
- 2 tablespoons honey
- 2 tablespoons soy sauce
- 2 teaspoons smoked paprika
- 1 teaspoon garlic powder
- 1 teaspoon dried oregano
- ½ teaspoon salt
- ½ teaspoon ground black pepper

Directions:
1. Preheat your air fryer to 200°C.
2. Rub the pork ribs with olive oil, honey, soy sauce, smoked paprika, garlic powder, oregano, salt, and pepper.
3. Place the pork ribs in the air fryer.
4. Cook for 25 minutes and serve immediately.

Nutritional values: Calories: 603; Total Fat: 36g; Carbohydrates: 17g; Protein: 44g.

Nutritional Values: Calories: 333, Fat: 23g, Carbohydrates: 2g, Protein: 27g

Air Fryer Lamb Chops

Preparation Time: 15 minutes
Cooking Time: 15 minutes
Number of Servings: 4

Ingredients:
- 4 lamb chops, trimmed and each weighing about 180g
- 2 tablespoons olive oil
- 2 tablespoons freshly chopped parsley
- 2 tablespoons freshly chopped rosemary
- 1 teaspoon dried oregano
- 1 teaspoon garlic powder
- Salt and freshly ground black pepper, to taste

Directions:
1. Preheat the air fryer to 200°C.
2. In a small bowl, mix together the olive oil, parsley, rosemary, oregano, garlic powder, salt, and pepper.
3. Rub the mixture onto the lamb chops, making sure to cover them completely.
4. Place the lamb chops into the air fryer basket and cook for 15 minutes, flipping halfway through.
5. Serve hot with your favorite sides.

Air Fryer Greek-Style Lamb Kebabs

Preparation Time: 10 minutes
Cooking Time: 10 minutes
Number of Servings: 4

Ingredients:
- 500g lamb mince
- 2 tablespoons olive oil
- 1 onion, finely chopped
- 2 cloves garlic, finely chopped
- 2 teaspoons dried oregano
- 2 teaspoons ground cumin
- 2 teaspoons ground coriander
- 2 teaspoons paprika
- Salt and freshly ground black pepper, to taste
- 8 wooden skewers, soaked in water for 10 minutes

Directions:
1. Preheat the air fryer to 180°C.
2. In a large bowl, mix together the lamb mince, olive oil, onion, garlic, oregano, cumin, coriander, paprika, salt, and pepper.
3. Separate the mixture into 8 equal parts and form each part into a kebab.
4. Thread each kebab onto a wooden skewer, making sure to press the mixture firmly onto the skewer.
5. Place the kebabs into the air fryer basket and cook for 10 minutes, flipping halfway through.
6. Serve hot with your favorite sides.

Nutritional Values: Calories: 286, Fat: 19g, Carbohydrates: 5g, Protein: 22g

Air Fryer Lamb Curry

Preparation Time: 10 minutes
Cooking Time: 20 minutes
Number of Servings: 4

Ingredients:
- 1 tablespoon olive oil
- 1 onion, finely chopped
- 2 cloves garlic, finely chopped
- 2 teaspoons freshly grated ginger
- 2 teaspoons ground cumin
- 2 teaspoons ground coriander
- 1 teaspoon ground turmeric
- 1 teaspoon ground cardamom
- 1 teaspoon chilli powder
- 500g lamb mince
- 1 can (400g) chopped tomatoes
- 2 tablespoons tomato paste
- 2 tablespoons freshly chopped coriander
- Salt and freshly ground black pepper, to taste

Directions:
1. Preheat the air fryer to 200°C.
2. Heat the olive oil in a large pan over medium heat. Add the onion and garlic and cook, stirring occasionally, until softened, about 5 minutes.
3. Add the ginger, cumin, coriander, turmeric, cardamom, and chilli powder and cook, stirring, for 1 minute.
4. Add the lamb mince and cook, breaking it up with a spoon, until no longer pink, about 5 minutes.
5. Add the chopped tomatoes, tomato paste, coriander, salt, and pepper and stir to combine.
6. Transfer the mixture to the air fryer basket and cook for 20 minutes, stirring halfway through.
7. Serve hot with your favorite sides.

Nutritional Values: Calories: 292, Fat: 16g, Carbohydrates: 12g, Protein: 22g

Air Fryer Lamb Roast

Preparation Time: 10 minutes
Cooking Time: 30 minutes
Number of Servings: 4

Ingredients:
- 1kg boneless leg of lamb
- 2 tablespoons olive oil
- 2 cloves garlic, minced
- 2 tablespoons freshly chopped rosemary
- 2 tablespoons freshly chopped thyme
- 2 teaspoons ground cumin
- Salt and freshly ground black pepper, to taste

Directions:
1. Preheat the air fryer to 200°C.
2. Rub the olive oil, garlic, rosemary, thyme, cumin, salt, and pepper onto the lamb, making sure to cover it completely.
3. Place the lamb into the air fryer basket and cook for 30 minutes, flipping halfway through.
4. Slice the lamb and serve hot with your favorite sides.

Nutritional Values: Calories: 205, Fat: 11g, Carbohydrates: 1g, Protein: 24g

Air Fryer Lamb Shanks

Preparation Time: 10 minutes
Cooking Time: 45 minutes
Number of Servings: 2

Ingredients:
- 2 Lamb Shanks
- 1 Tablespoon Olive Oil
- 1 Teaspoon Ground Cumin
- 1 Teaspoon Ground Cinnamon
- 1 Teaspoon Dried Oregano
- 1 Teaspoon Dried Thyme
- 1 Teaspoon Paprika
- Salt and Black Pepper to taste

Directions:
1. Preheat the air fryer to 200°C.
2. Pat the lamb shanks dry with paper towels.
3. In a small bowl, mix together the olive oil, cumin, cinnamon, oregano, thyme, and paprika.
4. Rub the spice mixture all over the lamb shanks, season with salt and pepper to taste.
5. Place the lamb shanks in the air fryer basket and cook for 45 minutes, flipping halfway through, until the lamb is cooked through and the outside is crispy and golden brown.
6. Serve the lamb shanks with your favorite accompaniments.

Nutritional Values: Calories: 174, Carbohydrates: 0.9g, Protein: 24.5g, Fat: 8.6g

Air Fryer Lamb and Sweet Potato Hash

Preparation Time: 10 minutes
Cooking Time: 25 minutes
Number of Servings: 4

Ingredients:
- 500g Lamb Mince
- 1 Teaspoon Dried Oregano
- 1 Teaspoon Dried Thyme
- Salt and Black Pepper to taste
- 2 Tablespoons Olive Oil
- 2 Sweet Potatoes, peeled and diced into cubes
- 1 Onion, finely chopped
- 2 Cloves Garlic, minced

Directions:
1. Preheat the air fryer to 200°C.
2. In a large bowl, mix together the lamb mince, oregano, thyme, salt, and pepper.
3. Heat the olive oil in a large pan over medium-high heat.
4. Add the sweet potatoes and cook for 5 minutes, stirring occasionally.
5. Add the onion and garlic and cook for another 5 minutes, stirring occasionally.
6. Add the lamb mince and cook for 10 minutes, stirring occasionally.
7. Transfer the lamb and sweet potato mixture to the air fryer basket and cook for 25 minutes, stirring occasionally, until the lamb is cooked through and the sweet potatoes are tender.
8. Serve the lamb and sweet potato hash with your favorite accompaniments.

Nutritional Values: Calories: 429, Carbohydrates: 27.3g, Protein: 24.5g, Fat: 25.7g

Air Fryer Lamb Meatballs

Preparation Time: 10 minutes
Cooking Time: 20 minutes
Number of Servings: 4

Ingredients:
- 500g Lean Lamb Mince
- 1 Egg
- 1 Tablespoon Dried Parsley
- 1 Teaspoon Ground Cumin
- 1 Teaspoon Ground Coriander
- Salt and Black Pepper to taste
- 2 Tablespoons Olive Oil

Directions:
1. Preheat the air fryer to 200°C.
2. In a large bowl, mix together the lamb mince, egg, parsley, cumin, coriander, salt, and pepper.
3. Form the mixture into 16 equal-sized meatballs.
4. Drizzle the olive oil over the meatballs and gently toss to coat.
5. Place the meatballs in the air fryer basket and cook for 20 minutes, flipping halfway through, until the meatballs are cooked through and crispy on the outside.
6. Serve the lamb meatballs with your favorite accompaniments.

Nutritional Values: Calories: 256, Carbohydrates: 0.9g, Protein: 22.4g, Fat: 17.1g

Air Fryer Lamb Burgers

Preparation Time: 5 minutes
Cooking Time: 10 minutes
Number of Servings: 4

Ingredients:
- 500g Lean Lamb Mince
- 1 Small Onion, finely chopped
- 1 Teaspoon Dried Oregano
- 1 Teaspoon Ground Cumin
- Salt and Black Pepper to taste
- 2 Tablespoons Olive Oil

Directions:
1. Preheat the air fryer to 200°C.
2. In a large bowl, mix together the lamb mince, onion, oregano, cumin, salt, and pepper.
3. Form the mixture into 4 equal-sized burgers.
4. Drizzle the olive oil over the burgers and gently toss to coat.
5. Place the burgers in the air fryer basket and cook for 10 minutes, flipping halfway through, until the burgers are cooked through and crispy on the outside.
6. Serve the lamb burgers with your favorite accompaniments.

Nutritional Values: Calories: 325, Carbohydrates: 1.2g, Protein: 24.1g, Fat: 22.6g

FISH AND SEAFOOD RECIPES

Air Fryer Fish and Chips

Preparation time: 10 minutes
Cooking time: 10 minutes
Number of servings: 2

Ingredients:
- 400g white fish fillets, skin removed
- 100g plain flour
- 1 teaspoon baking powder
- 1 teaspoon paprika
- Salt and pepper to taste
- 200ml lager beer
- 2 large potatoes, peeled and cut into chips
- 2 tablespoons vegetable oil

Directions:
1. Preheat air fryer to 200°C.
2. In a medium bowl, combine the flour, baking powder, paprika, salt and pepper.
3. Slowly pour in the lager beer and stir until a thick batter forms.
4. Dip the fish fillets in the batter, making sure they are completely coated.
5. Place the battered fish fillets in the preheated air fryer.
6. Cook for 10 minutes, turning once or twice during cooking.
7. Meanwhile, in a large bowl, toss the chips in the oil and season with salt and pepper.
8. Once the fish is cooked, add the chips to the air fryer.
9. Cook for a further 10 minutes, until the chips are golden brown.
10. Serve the fish and chips with your choice of sides.

Nutritional values: Calories: 616, Fat: 11.4g, Carbohydrates: 74.2g, Protein: 27.8g

Air Fryer Fish Fingers

Preparation Time: 10 minutes
Cooking Time: 10 minutes
Number of Servings: 4

Ingredients:
- 500g Fish Fingers
- 2 tablespoons Olive Oil
- Salt and Pepper to taste

Directions:
1. Preheat your air fryer to 190°C.
2. Place the fish fingers in a large bowl and drizzle with olive oil.
3. Sprinkle with salt and pepper to taste.
4. Place the fish fingers in the air fryer basket and cook for 10 minutes until golden and crispy.
5. Serve hot with your favorite sides.

Nutritional Values: Calories: 433, Protein: 24.2g, Fat: 30.2g, Carbohydrates: 2.5g, Fiber: 0.6g

Beer Battered Fish

Preparation Time: 10 minutes
Cooking Time: 10 minutes
Number of Servings: 4

Ingredients:
- 500g Fish Fillets
- 200ml Beer
- 120g Flour
- 2 tablespoons Olive Oil
- Salt and Pepper to taste

Directions:
1. Preheat your air fryer to 190°C.
2. In a bowl, mix together the beer and flour until a smooth batter forms.
3. Place the fish fillets in the batter and coat evenly.
4. Drizzle with olive oil and season with salt and pepper.
5. Place the fish fillets in the air fryer basket and cook for 10 minutes until golden and crispy.
6. Serve hot with your favorite sides.

Nutritional Values: Calories: 526, Protein: 33.2g, Fat: 14.2g, Carbohydrates: 52.2g, Fiber: 1.8g, Sugar: 1.1g

Air Fryer Salmon

Preparation Time: 10 minutes
Cooking Time: 10 minutes
Number of Servings: 4

Ingredients:
- 500g Salmon Fillets
- 2 tablespoons Olive Oil
- 2 tablespoons Lemon Juice
- Salt and Pepper to taste

Directions:
1. Preheat your air fryer to 190°C.
2. Place the salmon fillets in a large bowl and drizzle with olive oil and lemon juice.
3. Sprinkle with salt and pepper to taste.
4. Place the salmon fillets in the air fryer basket and cook for 10 minutes until golden and cooked through.
5. Serve hot with your favorite sides.

Nutritional Values: Calories: 442, Protein: 38.8g, Fat: 21.3g, Fiber: 0.3g

Air Fryer Fish Cakes

Preparation Time: 20 minutes
Cooking Time: 10 minutes
Number of Servings: 4

Ingredients:
- 400g white fish fillets, skinned and diced
- 1 large egg, lightly beaten
- 25g plain flour
- 2 tablespoons capers
- 1 tablespoon butter
- 2 cloves garlic, crushed
- 1 lemon, zested and juiced
- 2 tablespoons parsley, chopped
- Salt and pepper

- 2 tablespoons vegetable oil

Directions:
1. Place the fish into a bowl and season with salt and pepper.
2. In a separate bowl, mix together the egg, flour, capers, butter, garlic, lemon zest and juice, and parsley.
3. Add the egg mixture to the fish and mix until combined.
4. Heat the vegetable oil in the air fryer for 2 minutes.
5. Form the fish mixture into 4 patties and place in the air fryer.
6. Cook for 10 minutes, flipping the patties halfway through.
7. Serve with a side salad or potatoes

Nutritional Values: Calories: 211, Fat: 9.2g, Carbs: 9.3g, Protein: 21.7g

Air Fryer Fish Tacos

Preparation Time: 15 minutes
Cooking Time: 15 minutes
Number of Servings: 4

Ingredients:
- 400g white fish fillets, skinned and diced
- 2 tablespoons olive oil
- 2 tablespoons taco seasoning
- 8 small flour tortillas
- 200g shredded cabbage
- 2 avocados, sliced
- 2 limes, juiced
- 2 tablespoons cilantro, chopped
- 2 tablespoons sour cream
- 2 tablespoons salsa

Directions:
1. In a bowl, mix together the fish, olive oil and taco seasoning.
2. Place the fish in the air fryer and cook for 15 minutes, flipping halfway through.
3. Meanwhile, heat the tortillas in the oven for 5 minutes.
4. In a bowl, mix together the cabbage, avocados, lime juice and cilantro.

5. To assemble the tacos, fill the tortillas with the fish, cabbage mixture, sour cream and salsa.
6. Serve with extra cilantro, lime wedges and extra salsa.

Nutritional Values: Calories: 528, Fat: 28.2g, Carbs: 40.8g, Protein: 28.2g

Air Fryer Fish Pie

Preparation Time: 25 minutes
Cooking Time: 30 minutes
Number of Servings: 4

Ingredients:
- 400g white fish fillets, skinned and diced
- 2 tablespoons olive oil
- 1 onion, diced
- 2 cloves garlic, minced
- 150g mushrooms, sliced
- 200g frozen peas
- 2 tablespoons flour
- 400ml fish stock
- 2 tablespoons parsley, chopped
- 400g ready-made puff pastry
- 2 tablespoons milk

Directions:
1. Place the fish in the air fryer and cook for 10 minutes, flipping halfway through.
2. Meanwhile, heat the olive oil in a pan over medium heat. Add the onion and garlic and cook for 5 minutes.
3. Add the mushrooms and peas and cook for a further 5 minutes.

4. Sprinkle over the flour and cook for 1 minute.
5. Slowly pour in the fish stock and bring to a boil.
6. Reduce the heat and simmer for 5 minutes.
7. Stir in the parsley and cooked fish.
8. Preheat the air fryer to 200°C.
9. Grease a pie dish and pour in the fish mixture.
10. Cut the puff pastry into 4 equal pieces and cover the pie. Brush with the milk.
11. Place the pie in the air fryer and cook for 20 minutes, until the pastry is golden brown.

Nutritional Values: Calories: 632, Fat: 27.2g, Carbs: 58.1g, Protein: 32.9g

Air Fryer Panko Crusted Fish

Preparation Time: 10 minutes
Cooking Time: 8 minutes
Number of Servings: 4

Ingredients:
- 400g white fish fillets, skinned
- 2 eggs, lightly beaten
- 100g panko breadcrumbs
- 2 tablespoons Parmesan cheese, grated
- 2 tablespoons parsley, chopped
- Salt and pepper
- 2 tablespoons vegetable oil

Directions:
1. Place the fish fillets in a bowl and season with salt and pepper.
2. In a separate bowl, mix together the panko breadcrumbs, Parmesan cheese and parsley.
3. Dip each fillet into the egg, then the panko mixture, making sure to coat them evenly.
4. Heat the vegetable oil in the air fryer for 2 minutes.

5. Place the fillets in the air fryer and cook for 8 minutes, flipping halfway through.
6. Serve with a side salad or potatoes.

Nutritional Values: Calories: 309, Fat: 12.2g, Carbs: 14.7g, Protein: 33.8g

Air Fryer Fish Goujons

Preparation Time: 10 minutes
Cooking Time: 10 minutes
Number of Servings: 4

Ingredients:
- 400g of cod fillet, cut into strips
- 100g of plain flour
- 1 teaspoon of garlic powder
- 2 tablespoons of paprika
- 2 eggs, beaten
- 200g of bread crumbs

Directions:
1. Preheat the air fryer to 200°C.
2. In a shallow bowl, mix together the garlic powder and paprika.
3. Place the cod strips into the bowl and coat them in the seasoning.
4. Place the flour in a separate bowl and the eggs into another.
5. Dip each cod strip into the flour, then the eggs and finally the breadcrumbs.
6. Place the coated cod strips into the air fryer basket and cook for 10 minutes until golden.
7. Serve with your favorite accompaniments.

Nutritional Values: Calories: 333, Fat: 6.5g, Carbohydrates: 37.5g, Protein: 28.5g

Air Fryer Fish Goujons with Tartare Sauce

Preparation Time: 20 minutes
Cooking Time: 10 minutes
Number of Servings: 4

Ingredients:
- 400g of cod fillet, cut into strips
- 100g of plain flour
- 1 teaspoon of garlic powder
- 2 tablespoons of paprika
- 2 eggs, beaten
- 200g of bread crumbs
- 2 tablespoons of mayonnaise
- 1 tablespoon of capers
- 1 tablespoon of chopped fresh parsley
- 2 tablespoons of lemon juice

Directions:
1. Preheat the air fryer to 200°C.
2. In a shallow bowl, mix together the garlic powder and paprika.
3. Place the cod strips into the bowl and coat them in the seasoning.
4. Place the flour in a separate bowl and the eggs into another.
5. Dip each cod strip into the flour, then the eggs and finally the breadcrumbs.
6. Place the coated cod strips into the air fryer basket and cook for 10 minutes until golden.
7. Meanwhile, mix together the mayonnaise, capers, parsley and lemon juice to make a tartare sauce.
8. Serve the fish goujons with the tartare sauce and your favorite accompaniments.
Nutritional Values: Calories: 435, Fat: 12.5g, Carbohydrates: 41g, Protein: 33g

Air Fryer Seafood Paella

Preparation Time: 15 minutes
Cooking Time: 25 minutes
Number of Servings: 4

Ingredients:
- 500g of paella rice
- 1 red onion, finely chopped
- 2 cloves of garlic, minced
- 1 red pepper, diced
- 1 teaspoon of smoked paprika
- 400g of mixed seafood, such as prawns, mussels and squid
- 400ml of fish stock
- 2 tablespoons of olive oil
- 2 tablespoons of fresh parsley

Directions:
1. Preheat the air fryer to 200°C.
2. Heat the olive oil in a large frying pan over a medium heat.
3. Add the onion and garlic and cook for 5 minutes until softened.
4. Add the red pepper and smoked paprika and cook for a further 2 minutes.
5. Add the paella rice and mix to combine.
6. Pour over the fish stock and mix.
7. Transfer the mixture to the air fryer basket and cook for 20 minutes.
8. Add the mixed seafood to the paella and cook for a further 5 minutes until the seafood is cooked through.
9. Sprinkle with fresh parsley and serve.

Nutritional Values: Calories: 518, Fat: 11.5g, Carbohydrates: 68.5g, Protein: 28.5g

Air Fryer Coconut Crusted Fish

Preparation Time: 10 minutes
Cooking Time: 10 minutes
Number of Servings: 4

Ingredients:
- 400g of white fish fillets, such as cod or haddock
- 2 tablespoons of plain flour
- 2 eggs, beaten
- 200g of desiccated coconut
- 2 tablespoons of olive oil

Directions:
1. Preheat the air fryer to 200°C.
2. Place the flour into a shallow bowl and the beaten eggs into another.
3. Dip each fish fillet into the flour, then the eggs and finally the desiccated coconut.
4. Place the coated fish fillets into the air fryer basket and cook for 10 minutes until golden.
5. Serve with your favorite accompaniments.

Nutritional Values: Calories: 477, Fat: 28.5g, Carbohydrates: 22.5g, Protein: 33g

Air Fryer Shrimp Tempura

Preparation time: 15 minutes
Cooking time: 10 minutes
Number of servings: 4

Ingredients:
- 500g large raw shrimp, peeled and deveined
- 200g tempura batter mix
- 250 ml cold water
- Vegetable oil, for spraying

Directions:
1. Preheat the air fryer to 180°C.
2. In a large bowl, mix together the tempura batter mix and cold water until a smooth batter is formed.
3. Dip the shrimp in the batter, making sure they are completely coated.
4. Place the battered shrimp in the preheated air fryer basket and spray with a light coating of vegetable oil.
5. Cook for 10 minutes, until the shrimp is golden and crispy.
6. Serve immediately.

Nutritional values: Calories: 184, Carbohydrates: 24 g , Protein: 11 g, Fat: 4 g, Sodium: 437 mg

Air Fryer Fish Parcels

Preparation time: 15 minutes
Cooking time: 15 minutes
Number of servings: 4

Ingredients:
- 4 (200g each) white fish fillets
- 2 tablespoons olive oil
- 2 cloves garlic, minced
- 2 tablespoons fresh parsley, chopped
- 2 tablespoons butter
- 2 tablespoons lemon juice
- Salt and pepper, to taste

Directions:
1. Preheat the air fryer to 180°C.
2. In a small bowl, mix together the olive oil, garlic, parsley, butter, lemon juice, and salt and pepper.
3. Place the fish fillets in the preheated air fryer basket.
4. Divide the butter mixture evenly over each fish fillet and rub it in to ensure the fish is completely coated.
5. Place a piece of aluminum foil over each fish fillet and fold the edges to create a parcel.
6. Cook for 15 minutes, until the fish is cooked through.
7. Serve immediately.

Nutritional values: Calories: 250, Carbohydrates: 2g, Protein: 24g, Fat: 15g

Air Fryer Fish and Onion Rings

Preparation time: 15 minutes
Cooking time: 10 minutes
Number of servings: 4

Ingredients:
- 500g white fish fillets
- 250g onion rings
- 2 tablespoons olive oil
- Salt and pepper, to taste

Directions:
1. Preheat the air fryer to 180°C.
2. Place the fish fillets in the preheated air fryer basket and spray with a light coating of olive oil.
3. Place the onion rings on top of the fish fillets and spray with a light coating of olive oil.
4. Season with salt and pepper.
5. Cook for 10 minutes, until the fish and onion rings are golden and crispy.
6. Serve immediately.

Nutritional values: Calories: 256, Carbohydrates: 16 g, Protein: 22 g, Fat: 12 g, Sodium: 333 mg

Fish and Vegetable Skewers

Preparation time: 15 minutes
Cooking time: 15 minutes
Number of servings: 4

Ingredients:
- 500g white fish fillets
- 2 bell peppers, cut into pieces
- 1 red onion, cut into pieces
- 2 tablespoons olive oil
- Salt and pepper, to taste

Directions:
1. Preheat the air fryer to 180°C.
2. Cut the fish fillets into cubes and thread onto skewers, alternating with the bell pepper and red onion.
3. Place the skewers in the preheated air fryer basket and spray with a light coating of olive oil.
4. Season with salt and pepper.
5. Cook for 15 minutes, until the fish and vegetables are cooked through and golden.
6. Serve immediately.

Nutritional values: Calories: 218, Carbohydrates: 9 g, Protein: 25 g, Fat: 9 g

Air Fryer Fish Ceviche

Preparation time: 30 minutes
Cooking time: 10 minutes
Number of servings: 4

Ingredients:
- 500g white fish fillets, cut into small cubes
- 1 red onion, finely chopped
- 2 large tomatoes, diced
- 2 tablespoons freshly squeezed lime juice
- 1 tablespoon finely chopped fresh coriander
- 1 teaspoon chilli powder
- Salt and pepper to taste

Directions:
1. In a large bowl, combine the white fish cubes, red onion, tomatoes, lime juice, coriander, chilli powder, salt and pepper.
2. Mix well and set aside for 30 minutes.
3. Preheat the air fryer to 200°C.
4. Place the ceviche mixture in the air fryer basket and cook for 10 minutes.
5. Serve immediately.

Nutritional Values: Calories: 120, Fat: 2.5 g, Carbohydrates: 6 g, Protein: 16 g, Fiber: 1 g

Air Fryer Fish Burgers

Preparation time: 15 minutes
Cooking time: 10 minutes
Number of servings: 4

Ingredients:
- 500g white fish fillets, finely chopped
- 1 onion, finely chopped
- 2 tablespoons freshly chopped parsley
- 1 teaspoon ground paprika
- 1 teaspoon garlic powder
- 1 teaspoon cumin
- 2 tablespoons plain flour
- 2 tablespoons olive oil
- Salt and pepper to taste

Directions:
1. In a large bowl, combine the white fish, onion, parsley, paprika, garlic powder, cumin, flour, olive oil, salt and pepper.
2. Mix well and form the mixture into 4 patties.
3. Preheat the air fryer to 200°C (400°F).
4. Place the fish burgers in the air fryer basket and cook for 10 minutes.

5. Serve immediately.

Nutritional Values: Calories: 200, Fat: 8 g, Carbohydrates: 10 g, Protein: 22 g, Sodium: 200 mg, Fiber: 2 g

Air Fryer Fish with Lemon and Herb Butter

Preparation time: 10 minutes
Cooking time: 10 minutes
Number of servings: 4

Ingredients:
- 500g white fish fillets
- 2 tablespoons butter, softened
- 2 tablespoons freshly chopped parsley
- 1 teaspoon garlic powder
- 1 teaspoon dried oregano
- 1 teaspoon lemon zest
- Salt and pepper to taste

Directions:
1. In a small bowl, combine the butter, parsley, garlic powder, oregano, lemon zest, salt and pepper.
2. Mix well, then spread the mixture over the white fish fillets.
3. Preheat the air fryer to 200°C.
4. Place the fish fillets in the air fryer basket and cook for 10 minutes.
5. Serve immediately.

Nutritional Values: Calories: 200, Fat: 9 g, Carbohydrates: 1 g, Protein: 28 g, Fiber: 0 g

Air Fryer Calamari Fries

Preparation Time: 10 minutes
Cooking Time: 8 minutes
Number of Servings: 4

Ingredients:
- 800g of squid, cut into strips
- 2 tablespoons of olive oil
- 2 tablespoons of fresh parsley, finely chopped
- 2 cloves of garlic, crushed
- 2 tablespoons of lemon juice
- 200g of breadcrumbs
- 2 teaspoons of paprika
- Salt and pepper, to taste

Directions:
1. Preheat your air fryer to 200°C.
2. In a medium bowl, mix together the olive oil, parsley, garlic, lemon juice, breadcrumbs, paprika, salt, and pepper.
3. Dip the squid strips into the olive oil mixture and coat each one evenly.
4. Place the squid strips into the air fryer basket and cook for 8 minutes.
5. Serve the calamari with some lemon wedges and enjoy!

Nutritional Values: Calories: 200, Fat: 7g, Carbohydrates: 20g, Protein: 11g

SIDES RECIPES

Air Fryer Roast Potatoes

Preparation Time: 10 mins
Cooking Time: 25 mins
Number of Servings: 4

Ingredients:
- 4 large potatoes, peeled and cut into small chunks
- 4 tablespoons of vegetable oil
- 2 teaspoons of dried rosemary
- 1 teaspoon of garlic powder
- ½ teaspoon of black pepper
- ½ teaspoon of salt

Directions:
1. Preheat the air fryer to 200°C (400°F).
2. Place the potato chunks into a large bowl and drizzle with the oil.
3. Add the rosemary, garlic powder, pepper and salt, then mix until the potatoes are evenly coated.
4. Place the potatoes into the air fryer basket and cook for 25 minutes, shaking the basket every 5 minutes to ensure even cooking.
5. Serve hot.

Nutritional Values: Calories: 200, Fat: 10g, Carbohydrates: 24g, Protein: 4g, Fiber: 2g

Air Fryer Chips

Preparation Time: 10 mins
Cooking Time: 25 mins
Number of Servings: 4

Ingredients:
- 4 large potatoes, peeled and cut into chips
- 4 tablespoons of vegetable oil
- 1 teaspoon of salt
- ½ teaspoon of black pepper

Directions:
1. Preheat the air fryer to 200°C.
2. Place the potato chips into a large bowl and drizzle with the oil.
3. Add the salt and pepper, then mix until the potatoes are evenly coated.
4. Place the chips into the air fryer basket and cook for 25 minutes, shaking the basket every 5 minutes to ensure even cooking.
5. Serve hot.

Nutritional Values: Calories: 200, Fat: 10g, Carbohydrates: 24g, Protein: 4g, Fiber: 2g

Air Fryer Baked Beans

Preparation Time: 10 mins
Cooking Time: 20 mins
Number of Servings: 4

Ingredients:

- 2 (400g) cans of baked beans
- 2 tablespoons of brown sugar
- 1 teaspoon of garlic powder
- ½ teaspoon of smoked paprika

Directions:
1. Preheat the air fryer to 180°C.
2. Place the beans into a medium sized bowl and add the brown sugar, garlic powder and smoked paprika.
3. Mix the ingredients until the beans are evenly coated.
4. Place the beans into the air fryer basket and cook for 20 minutes, shaking the basket every 5 minutes to ensure even cooking.
5. Serve hot.

Nutritional Values: Calories: 200, Fat: 2g, Carbohydrates: 34g, Protein: 9g, Fiber: 5g

Air Fryer Garlic Bread

Preparation Time: 10 mins
Cooking Time: 8 mins
Number of Servings: 4

Ingredients:
- 4 slices of white bread
- 2 tablespoons of butter, melted
- 2 cloves of garlic, minced
- 2 tablespoons of fresh parsley, chopped

Directions:
1. Preheat the air fryer to 200°C.
2. Place the bread slices onto a cutting board.
3. In a small bowl, stir together the melted butter, garlic and parsley.
4. Brush the butter mixture onto the bread slices.
5. Place the bread slices into the air fryer basket and cook for 8 minutes, flipping the slices halfway through.
6. Serve hot.

Nutritional Values: Calories: 200, Fat: 10g, Carbohydrates: 24g, Protein: 4g, Fiber: 1g

Cheese & Bacon Balls

Preparation Time: 10 minutes
Cooking Time: 10 minutes
Servings: 4

Ingredients:
- 200g bacon, diced
- 200g cheddar cheese, grated
- 2 tablespoons chopped fresh parsley
- 2 eggs
- 50g plain flour
- 2 tablespoons olive oil

Directions:
1. Preheat your air fryer to 200°C.
2. In a large bowl combine the bacon, cheese, and parsley.
3. In a separate bowl, beat the eggs.
4. Add the flour to the egg mixture and stir to combine.
5. Add the egg mixture to the bacon mixture and stir to combine.
6. Form the mixture into small balls, about 2 cm in diameter.
7. Place the balls in the air fryer basket and spray with the olive oil.
8. Cook for 10 minutes, or until golden brown and crispy.

Nutritional Values: Calories: 394 kcal, Carbohydrates: 6.4 g, Protein: 17.8 g, Fat: 32.3 g

Air Fryer Corn on the Cob

Preparation time: 5 minutes
Cooking time: 15 minutes
Number of servings: 4

Ingredients:
- 4 ears of corn (shucked, with husks removed)
- 1 tablespoon (15ml) vegetable oil
- Salt and pepper to taste

Directions:
1. Preheat the air fryer to 200°C.
2. Place the ears of corn in the air fryer basket and spray with the vegetable oil.
3. Sprinkle the corn with salt and pepper to taste.
4. Place the corn in the air fryer and cook for 15 minutes, shaking the basket every 5 minutes.
5. Remove the corn from the air fryer and serve hot.

Nutritional values: Calories: 130, Carbohydrates: 27g, Protein: 4g, Fat: 2g, Sodium: 10mg, Fiber: 2g

Yorkshire Puddings

Preparation time: 10 minutes

Cooking time: 20 minutes
Number of servings: 4

Ingredients:
- 150g plain flour
- 3 eggs
- 150ml milk
- 1 tablespoon (15ml) vegetable oil
- Salt and pepper to taste

Directions:
1. Preheat the air fryer to 200°C.
2. In a large bowl, whisk together the flour, eggs, milk, vegetable oil, salt and pepper until smooth.
3. Grease 4 individual muffin tins with vegetable oil and fill each tin with the batter.
4. Place the tins in the air fryer and cook for 20 minutes, shaking the basket every 5 minutes.
5. Remove the Yorkshire puddings from the air fryer and serve hot.

Nutritional values: Calories: 144 kcal, Carbohydrates: 15g, Protein: 7g, Fat: 6g, Sodium: 98mg, Fiber: 1g

Sweet Potato Fries

Preparation time: 10 minutes
Cooking time: 15 minutes
Number of servings: 4

Ingredients:
2 large sweet potatoes, peeled and cut into fries
2 tablespoons (30ml) vegetable oil
Salt and pepper to taste

Directions:
1. Preheat the air fryer to 200°C.
2. Place the sweet potato fries in a large bowl and toss with the vegetable oil, salt and pepper.
3. Place the fries in the air fryer and cook for 15 minutes, shaking the basket every 5 minutes.

4. Remove the fries from the air fryer and serve hot.

Nutritional values: Calories: 157, Carbohydrates: 22g, Protein: 2g, Fat: 8g, Sodium: 23mg, Fiber: 3g

Air Fryer Potato Wedges

Preparation time: 10 minutes
Cooking time: 15 minutes
Number of servings: 4

Ingredients:
- 4 medium-sized potatoes
- 2 tablespoons olive oil
- 2 teaspoons salt
- 1 teaspoon paprika
- 1 teaspoon garlic powder

Directions:
1. Preheat air fryer to 200°C.
2. Wash and peel the potatoes, then cut them into wedges.
3. Place the potato wedges in a bowl and add the olive oil, salt, paprika, and garlic powder. Mix well until the wedges are evenly coated.
4. Place the wedges in the air fryer basket and cook for 15 minutes, flipping them over halfway through.
5. Serve hot with ketchup or your favorite dip.

Nutritional Values: Calories: 178, Fat: 6.2g, Carbohydrates: 28.6g, Protein: 3.2g

Air Fryer Mushrooms

Preparation time: 5 minutes
Cooking time: 10 minutes
Number of servings: 4

Ingredients:
- 500g mushrooms, sliced
- 2 tablespoons olive oil
- 1 teaspoon salt
- 1 teaspoon ground black pepper

Directions:
1. Preheat air fryer to 200°C.
2. Place the mushrooms in a bowl and add the olive oil, salt, and pepper. Mix well until the mushrooms are evenly coated.
3. Place the mushrooms in the air fryer basket and cook for 10 minutes, flipping them over halfway through.
4. Serve hot as a side dish or snack.

Nutritional Values: Calories: 91, Fat: 7.1g, Carbohydrates: 5.2g, Protein: 3.6g

Air Fryer Baked Apples

Preparation time: 10 minutes
Cooking time: 15 minutes
Number of servings: 4

Ingredients:
- 4 medium-sized apples

- 2 tablespoons brown sugar
- 1 teaspoon ground cinnamon
- 1 teaspoon ground nutmeg
- 2 tablespoons butter, melted

Directions:
1. Preheat air fryer to 200°C.
2. Wash and core the apples, then cut them into wedges.
3. Place the apple wedges in a bowl and add the brown sugar, cinnamon, nutmeg, and melted butter. Mix well until the wedges are evenly coated.
4. Place the wedges in the air fryer basket and cook for 15 minutes, flipping them over halfway through.
5. Serve warm with ice cream or your favorite topping.

Nutritional Values: Calories: 177, Fat: 8.3g, Carbohydrates: 26.4g, Protein: 0.8g

Air Fryer Scotch Eggs

Preparation time: 10 minutes
Cooking time: 10 minutes
Number of servings: 4

Ingredients:
- 4 large eggs
- 200g pork sausage meat
- 1 teaspoon salt
- 1 teaspoon ground black pepper
- 2 tablespoons olive oil

Directions:
1. Preheat air fryer to 200°C.
2. Hard-boil the eggs, then peel and set aside.
3. In a bowl, mix together the sausage meat, salt, pepper, and olive oil.
4. Divide the sausage mixture into 4 equal parts and flatten into patties.
5. Wrap each egg in one of the sausage patties and press to seal.
6. Place the Scotch eggs in the air fryer basket and cook for 10 minutes, flipping them over halfway through.
7. Serve hot as a snack or starter.

Nutritional Values: Calories: 415, Fat: 30.8g, Carbohydrates: 3.2g, Protein: 25.2g

Cheese & Herb Croquettes

Preparation time: 10 minutes
Cooking time: 15 minutes
Number of servings: 4

Ingredients:
- 200g grated cheese
- 2 large eggs
- 1/4 teaspoon garlic powder
- 1/4 teaspoon dried oregano
- 1/4 teaspoon dried basil
- 1/4 teaspoon dried thyme
- 150g plain flour
- 2 tablespoons olive oil
- Salt and pepper to taste

Directions:
1. In a large bowl, combine the grated cheese, eggs, garlic powder, oregano, basil, thyme, flour, olive oil, and salt and pepper. Stir all ingredients together until a dense mixture forms.
2. Using a tablespoon, scoop out the batter and shape it into small croquettes. Place them on a plate or baking tray in the refrigerator for 10 minutes.
3. Preheat your air fryer to 200°C.
4. Add the croquettes to the air fryer basket and cook for 15 minutes, or until golden brown and crispy.

5. Serve the croquettes with your favorite dipping sauce. Enjoy!

Nutritional Values: Calories: 194, Carbohydrates: 11.9g, Protein: 8.6g, , Fat: 11.2g

Nutritional Values: Calories: 190, Fat: 7g, Carbohydrates: 25g, Protein: 4g

Air Fryer Vegetable Pakoras

Preparation Time: 10 minutes
Cooking Time: 15 minutes
Number of Servings: 4

Ingredients:
- 250g potatoes, peeled and grated
- 150g onion, grated
- 75g carrots, grated
- 75g courgettes, grated
- 2 cloves of garlic, minced
- 2 tablespoons fresh coriander, chopped
- 1 tablespoon fresh ginger, grated
- 2 tablespoons gram flour
- 1 teaspoon chilli powder
- 1 teaspoon cumin powder
- 1 teaspoon garam masala
- Salt and pepper to taste
- 2 tablespoons vegetable oil
- 100g gram flour for coating
- Oil for air frying

Directions:
1. In a large bowl, combine the potatoes, onion, carrots, courgettes, garlic, coriander, ginger, gram flour, chilli powder, cumin powder, garam masala, salt, pepper and vegetable oil. Mix until all ingredients are combined.
2. Form the mixture into small patties and coat them in gram flour.
3. Preheat the air fryer to 200°C.
4. Place the coated patties into the air fryer and cook for 12-15 minutes, flipping them halfway through.
5. When the pakoras are golden-brown, remove them from the air fryer and serve hot.

Carrot & Parsnip Fries

Preparation Time: 10 minutes
Cooking Time: 20 minutes
Number of Servings: 4

Ingredients:
- 500g carrots, peeled and cut into fries
- 500g parsnips, peeled and cut into fries
- 2 tablespoons olive oil
- 2 teaspoons garlic powder
- 2 teaspoons paprika
- 1 teaspoon ground black pepper
- Salt to taste
- 2 tablespoons fresh parsley, chopped

Directions:
1. In a large bowl, combine the carrots, parsnips, olive oil, garlic powder, paprika, black pepper and salt. Mix until all ingredients are combined.
2. Preheat the air fryer to 200°C.
3. Place the fries into the air fryer and cook for 15-20 minutes, flipping them halfway through.

4. When the fries are golden-brown, remove them from the air fryer and sprinkle with the chopped parsley. Serve hot.

Nutritional Values: Calories: 224 , Fat: 5g , Carbohydrates: 39g, Protein: 5g

VEGETARIAN RECIPES

Air Fryer Halloumi Fries

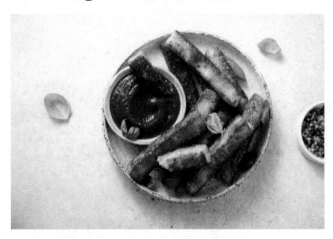

Preparation time: 10 minutes
Cooking time: 12 minutes
Number of servings: 2

Ingredients:
- 200g halloumi cheese, cut into fries
- 2 tablespoons olive oil
- 1 teaspoon dried oregano
- 1 teaspoon ground cumin
- 1/2 teaspoon garlic powder
- 1/2 teaspoon paprika
- Salt and pepper, to taste

Directions:
1. Preheat the air fryer to 200°C.
2. Cut the halloumi cheese into fries.
3. In a large bowl, combine the halloumi fries with the olive oil, oregano, cumin, garlic powder, paprika, salt and pepper.
4. Place the fries in the air fryer basket and cook for 12 minutes, or until golden brown.
5. Serve hot.

Nutritional Values: Calories: 497, Fat: 35.2 g, Carbohydrates: 8.2 g, Protein: 35.2 g

Air Fryer Falafel

Preparation time: 10 minutes
Cooking time: 15 minutes
Number of servings: 4

Ingredients:
- 400g canned chickpeas, drained
- 1/2 onion, finely chopped
- 2 cloves garlic, minced
- 60g of fresh parsley, chopped
- 1 teaspoon ground cumin
- 1/2 teaspoon ground coriander
- 1/2 teaspoon baking powder
- 2 tablespoons all-purpose flour
- Salt and pepper, to taste

Directions:
1. Preheat the air fryer to 200°C.
2. In a food processor, combine the chickpeas, onion, garlic, parsley, cumin, coriander, baking powder, flour, salt and pepper. Pulse until it forms a paste.
3. Form the paste into walnut-sized balls.
4. Place the falafel balls in the air fryer basket and cook for 15 minutes, or until golden brown.
5. Serve with hummus and tzatziki.

Nutritional Values: Calories: 272, Fat: 8.7 g, Carbohydrates: 32.2 g, Protein: 14.6 g

Sweet Potato Chips

Preparation time: 10 minutes

Cooking time: 20 minutes
Number of servings: 4

Ingredients:
- 4 large sweet potatoes, cut into chips
- 2 tablespoons olive oil
- 1 teaspoon garlic powder
- 1 teaspoon paprika
- 1/2 teaspoon dried oregano
- Salt and pepper, to taste

Directions:
1. Preheat the air fryer to 200°C.
2. In a large bowl, combine the sweet potato chips with the olive oil, garlic powder, paprika, oregano, salt and pepper.
3. Place the sweet potato chips in the air fryer basket and cook for 20 minutes, or until golden brown.
4. Serve hot with your favorite dip.

Nutritional Values: Calories: 199, Fat: 7.8 g, Carbohydrates: 31.9 g, Protein: 2.3 g

Air Fryer Carrot Fries

Preparation time: 10 minutes
Cooking time: 15 minutes
Number of servings: 4

Ingredients:
- 500g carrots, peeled and cut into sticks
- 2 tablespoons olive oil
- 1 teaspoon garlic powder
- 1 teaspoon smoked paprika
- Salt and pepper to taste

Directions:
1. Preheat the air fryer to 190°C.
2. Place the carrot sticks in a bowl and add olive oil, garlic powder, smoked paprika, salt and pepper.
Mix everything together until the carrots are evenly coated.

3. Place the carrot sticks in the air fryer basket in a single layer and cook for 15 minutes at 190°C, shaking the basket every 5 minutes.
4. Serve the carrot fries warm.

Nutritional Values: Calories: 126, Total Fat: 7.4g, Carbohydrates: 13.4g, Fiber: 3.6g, Protein: 1.3g

Air Fryer Butternut Squash Fries

Preparation time: 10 minutes
Cooking time: 15 minutes
Number of servings: 4

Ingredients:
- 500g butternut squash, peeled and cut into sticks
- 2 tablespoons olive oil
- 1 teaspoon garlic powder
- 1 teaspoon dried thyme
- Salt and pepper to taste

Directions:
1. Preheat the air fryer to 190°C.
2. Place the butternut squash in a bowl and add olive oil, garlic powder, dried thyme, salt and pepper.

Mix everything together until the butternut squash is evenly coated.

3. Place the butternut squash sticks in the air fryer basket in a single layer and cook for 15 minutes at 190°C, shaking the basket every 5 minutes.
4. Serve the butternut squash fries warm.

Nutritional Values: Calories: 126, Fat: 7.4g , Carbohydrates: 13.2g, Fiber: 3.5g, Protein: 1.4g

Air Fryer Zucchini Chips

Preparation time: 10 minutes
Cooking time: 10 minutes
Number of servings: 4

Ingredients:
- 500g zucchini, sliced into thin rounds
- 2 tablespoons olive oil
- 1 teaspoon garlic powder
- 1 teaspoon dried oregano
- Salt and pepper to taste

Directions:
1. Preheat the air fryer to 190°C.
2. Place the zucchini slices in a bowl and add olive oil, garlic powder, dried oregano, salt and pepper. Mix everything together until the zucchini is evenly coated.
3. Place the zucchini slices in the air fryer basket in a single layer and cook for 10 minutes at 190°C, shaking the basket every 5 minutes.
4. Serve the zucchini chips warm.

Nutritional Values: Calories: 126, Fat: 7.4g, Carbohydrates: 13.4g, Fiber: 2.9g, Protein: 1.4g

Air Fryer Veggie Burgers

Preparation time: 10 minutes
Cooking time: 15 minutes
Number of servings: 4

Ingredients:
- 500g sweet potato, peeled and grated
- 1 small onion, diced
- 2 cloves garlic, minced
- 2 tablespoons olive oil
- 1 teaspoon ground cumin
- 1 teaspoon smoked paprika
- 1 teaspoon dried oregano
- Salt and pepper to taste

Directions:
1. Preheat the air fryer to 190°C.
2. In a large bowl, combine the grated sweet potato, onion, garlic, olive oil, cumin, smoked paprika, oregano, salt and pepper. Mix everything together until everything is evenly combined.
3. Shape the mixture into 4 patties and place them in the air fryer basket in a single layer. Cook for 15 minutes at 190°C, flipping halfway through.
4. Serve the veggie burgers warm.

Nutritional Values: Calories: 126, Fat: 7.4g, Carbohydrates: 13.4g, Fiber: 2.6g, Protein: 1.4g

Air Fryer Roasted Brussels Sprouts

Preparation time: 10 minutes
Cooking time: 15 minutes
Number of servings: 4

Ingredients:
- 500 g Brussels sprouts, trimmed and halved
- 2 tablespoons olive oil
- Salt and pepper, to taste

Directions:
1. Preheat the air fryer to 180ºC.
2. Place the Brussels sprouts in the air fryer basket and drizzle with the olive oil. Season with salt and pepper.
3. Cook in the air fryer for 15 minutes, shaking halfway through cooking.
4. Serve hot.

Nutritional values: Calories: 94, Fat: 5.4 g, Carbohydrates: 8.4 g, Fiber: 3.2 g

Air Fryer Eggplant Parmesan

Preparation time: 20 minutes
Cooking time: 25 minutes
Number of servings: 4

Ingredients:
- 2 medium eggplants, sliced into 1.5 cm rounds
- 120g of all-purpose flour
- 2 large eggs, beaten
- 250g of seasoned bread crumbs
- 80g of grated Parmesan cheese
- 1/4 teaspoon dried oregano
- 1/4 teaspoon garlic powder
- 1/4 teaspoon sea salt
- 1/4 teaspoon freshly ground black pepper
- 120g marinara sauce
- 120g shredded mozzarella cheese

Directions:
1. Preheat the air fryer to 200°C.
2. Place the flour in a shallow bowl. Put the eggs in a separate shallow bowl. In a third shallow bowl, combine the bread crumbs, Parmesan cheese, oregano, garlic powder, salt and pepper.
3. Dip each eggplant slice in the flour, then the egg, and then the bread crumb mixture.
4. Place the eggplant slices in the air fryer basket and cook for 8 minutes. Flip the eggplant slices and cook for an additional 8 minutes.
5. Remove the eggplant slices from the air fryer and spread a layer of marinara sauce over the top of each slice. Sprinkle with mozzarella cheese.
6. Return the slices to the air fryer and cook for an additional 5 minutes, until the cheese is melted and bubbly.
7. Serve hot.

Nutritional values: Calories: 259, Fat: 12g, Carbohydrates: 27g, Protein: 11g

Air Fryer Broccoli and Cauliflower

Preparation time: 10 minutes
Cooking time: 15 minutes
Number of servings: 4

Ingredients:
- 450g broccoli florets

- 450g cauliflower florets
- 2 tablespoons olive oil
- 1 teaspoon sea salt
- 1 teaspoon freshly ground black pepper

Directions:
1. Preheat the air fryer to 200°C.
2. Place the broccoli and cauliflower florets in the air fryer basket and drizzle with the olive oil. Sprinkle with salt and pepper.
3. Cook in the air fryer for 15 minutes, stirring occasionally, until golden brown and crispy.
4. Serve hot.

Nutritional values: Calories: 94, Fat: 7g, Carbohydrates: 7g, Protein: 4g

Air Fryer Asparagus Spears

Preparation time: 10 minutes
Cooking time: 10 minutes
Number of servings: 4

Ingredients:
- 450g asparagus spears, trimmed
- 2 tablespoons olive oil
- 1 teaspoon sea salt
- 1 teaspoon freshly ground black pepper

Directions:

1. Preheat the air fryer to 200°C.
2. Place the asparagus spears in the air fryer basket and drizzle with the olive oil. Sprinkle with salt and pepper.
3. Cook in the air fryer for 10 minutes, stirring occasionally, until golden brown and crispy.
4. Serve hot.

Nutritional values: Calories: 49, Fat: 4g, Carbohydrates: 4g, Protein: 3g

Air Fryer Portobello Mushrooms

Preparation time: 10 minutes
Cooking time: 10 minutes
Number of servings: 2

Ingredients:
- 2 large portobello mushrooms
- 2 tbsp olive oil
- 1/2 tsp garlic powder
- 1/2 tsp onion powder
- 1/2 tsp sea salt
- 1/2 tsp black pepper
- 2 tbsp chopped fresh parsley

Directions:
1. Preheat air fryer to 200°C.
2. In a medium bowl, combine the olive oil, garlic powder, onion powder, sea salt, and black pepper.
3. Dip the mushrooms in the mixture, coating them completely.
4. Place the mushrooms in the air fryer basket and cook for 10 minutes, flipping the mushrooms halfway through.
5. Sprinkle with the chopped parsley and serve.

Nutritional Values: Calories: 162, Fat: 12.8 g, Carbohydrates: 4.2 g, Protein: 4.2 g

Air Fryer Tofu Nuggets

Preparation time: 10 minutes
Cooking time: 10 minutes
Number of servings: 2

Ingredients:
- 200 g firm tofu, cut into nugget-size pieces
- 120g of breadcrumbs
- 60g of grated Parmesan cheese
- 1/2 tsp garlic powder
- 1/2 tsp onion powder
- 1/2 tsp sea salt
- 1/2 tsp black pepper
- 2 tbsp olive oil

Directions:
1. Preheat air fryer to 200°C.
2. In a shallow bowl, combine the breadcrumbs, Parmesan cheese, garlic powder, onion powder, sea salt, and black pepper.
3. Dip the tofu nuggets in the mixture, coating them completely.
4. Place the nuggets in the air fryer basket and drizzle with the olive oil.
5. Cook for 10 minutes, flipping the nuggets halfway through.

Nutritional Values: Calories: 236, Fat: 14.4 g, Carbohydrates: 14.1 g, Protein: 13.4 g

Air Fryer Rice and Beans

Preparation time: 10 minutes
Cooking time: 10 minutes
Number of servings: 2

Ingredients:
- 250g of cooked white rice
- 250g of cooked black beans
- 1/2 tsp garlic powder
- 1/2use only grams
- ½ tsp onion powder
- 1/2 tsp sea salt
- 1/2 tsp black pepper
- 2 tbsp olive oil

Directions:
1. Preheat air fryer to 200°C.
2. In a medium bowl, combine the cooked white rice, cooked black beans, garlic powder, onion powder, sea salt, and black pepper.
3. Drizzle the olive oil over the mixture and stir to combine.
4. Place the mixture in the air fryer basket and cook for 10 minutes, stirring halfway through.

Nutritional Values: Calories: 307, Fat: 10.8 g, Carbohydrates: 36.7 g, Protein: 11.7 g

Veggie Quesadillas

Preparation time: 10 minutes
Cooking time: 10 minutes

Number of servings: 2

Ingredients:
- 2 large flour tortillas
- 250g of grated cheese
- 120g of cooked black beans
- 120g of diced bell peppers
- 120g of diced red onion
- 2 tbsp chopped fresh cilantro
- 2 tbsp olive oil

Directions:
1. Preheat air fryer to 200°C.
2. Place one tortilla on a cutting board and sprinkle with half of the grated cheese, black beans, bell peppers, red onion, and cilantro.
3. Top with the other tortilla and brush both sides with olive oil.
4. Place the quesadilla in the air fryer basket and cook for 10 minutes, flipping halfway through.
5. Cut into slices and serve.

Nutritional Values: Calories: 429, Fat: 22.3 g, Carbohydrates: 37.3 g, Protein: 17.3 g

Spinach Artichoke Dip

Preparation time: 10 minutes
Cooking time: 10 minutes
Number of servings: 4

Ingredients:
- 400g frozen spinach
- 200g canned artichoke hearts
- 3 cloves garlic, minced
- 2 tablespoons olive oil
- 1 teaspoon ground nutmeg
- 2 teaspoons lemon juice
- 220ml Greek yoghurt
- 220ml crème fraîche
- 200g grated Parmesan cheese
- Salt and pepper, to taste

Directions:
1. Preheat the air fryer to 180°C.

2. In a medium bowl, combine the spinach, artichoke hearts, garlic, olive oil, nutmeg, lemon juice, yoghurt, crème fraîche, and Parmesan cheese.
3. Mix until all ingredients are evenly combined.
4. Place the dip in the air fryer basket, and cook for 10 minutes.
5. Serve warm with crackers or tortilla chips.

Nutritional values: Calories: 372, Fat: 25.2g, Carbohydrates: 13.9g, Protein: 21.4g

Air Fryer Potato Skins

Preparation time: 10 minutes
Cooking time: 10 minutes
Number of servings: 4

Ingredients:
- 4 medium potatoes
- 2 tablespoons olive oil
- 2 cloves garlic, minced
- 1 teaspoon smoked paprika
- 2 tablespoons fresh parsley, chopped
- 150g grated cheddar cheese
- Salt and pepper, to taste

Directions:
1. Preheat the air fryer to 200°C.
2. Wash and dry the potatoes, then prick them with a fork.

3. Brush the potatoes with olive oil, then place them in the air fryer basket.
4. Cook for 10 minutes, or until the potatoes are cooked through.
5. Remove the potatoes from the air fryer, and slice them in half.
6. Scoop out the flesh of the potatoes, leaving a layer of potato around the skin.
7. Place the potato skins back in the air fryer basket and cook for a further 5 minutes.
8. Meanwhile, in a small bowl, combine the garlic, paprika, parsley, cheddar cheese, salt, and pepper.
9. Remove the potato skins from the air fryer and fill with the cheese mixture.
10. Return the potato skins to the air fryer and cook for a further 5 minutes.
11. Serve hot.

Nutritional values: Calories: 300, Fat: 13.4g, Carbohydrates: 30.9g, Protein: 13.4g

Cauliflower Bites

Preparation time: 10 minutes
Cooking time: 10 minutes
Number of servings: 4

Ingredients:
- 600g cauliflower, cut into florets
- 2 tablespoons olive oil
- 2 cloves garlic, minced
- 1 teaspoon paprika
- 1 teaspoon ground cumin
- 2 tablespoons fresh parsley, chopped
- Salt and pepper, to taste

Directions:
1. Preheat the air fryer to 180°C.
2. In a medium bowl, combine the cauliflower florets, olive oil, garlic, paprika, cumin, parsley, salt, and pepper.
3. Mix until all ingredients are evenly combined.
4. Place the cauliflower in the air fryer basket, and cook for 10 minutes.

5. Serve hot.

Nutritional values: Calories: 151, Fat: 9.1g, Carbohydrates: 10.8g, Protein: 5.9g

Air Fryer Veggie Nachos

Preparation time: 10 minutes
Cooking time: 10 minutes
Number of servings: 4

Ingredients:
- 2 large potatoes, thinly sliced
- 2 tablespoons olive oil
- 1 red onion, diced
- 1 red pepper, diced
- 2 cloves garlic, minced
- 1 teaspoon smoked paprika
- 2 tablespoons fresh parsley, chopped
- 150g grated cheddar cheese
- Salt and pepper, to taste

Directions:
1. Preheat the air fryer to 200°C.
2. In a medium bowl, combine the potatoes, olive oil, onion, red pepper, garlic, paprika, parsley, salt, and pepper.
3. Mix until all ingredients are evenly combined.
4. Place the potatoes in the air fryer basket and cook for 10 minutes.
5. Remove the potatoes from the air fryer and top with the grated cheese.
6. Return the potatoes to the air fryer and cook for a further 5 minutes and serve.

Nutritional values: Calories: 441, Fat: 22.4g, Carbohydrates: 42.3g, Protein: 17.6g

SNACKS & APPETIZERS

Air Fryer Onion Rings

Preparation time: 10 minutes
Cooking time: 8 minutes
Number of servings: 2

Ingredients:
- 2 large onions, peeled and cut into rings
- 2 tablespoons olive oil
- 2 tablespoons cornflour
- 2 tablespoons plain flour
- 1 teaspoon paprika
- 1 teaspoon garlic powder
- Salt and pepper, to taste
- Oil, for spraying

Directions:
1. Preheat the air fryer to 180°C.
2. In a large bowl, combine the olive oil, cornflour, plain flour, paprika, garlic powder, salt and pepper.
3. Add the onion rings and mix until evenly coated.
4. Place the onion rings in the air fryer basket and spray with oil.
5. Cook for 8 minutes, shaking the basket occasionally.

Nutritional values: Calories: 222, Fat: 10g, Carbohydrates: 28g, Protein: 5g

Air Fryer Baked Potatoes

Preparation time: 10 minutes
Cooking time: 30-40 minutes
Number of servings: 4

Ingredients:
- 4 large potatoes, peeled and washed (800g)
- 2 tablespoons olive oil (30ml)
- Salt and pepper to taste

Directions:
1. Preheat the air fryer to 200°C.
2. Cut the potatoes into halves.
3. Place the potatoes into a large bowl and drizzle with olive oil.
4. Season with salt and pepper.
5. Place the potatoes into the air fryer basket.
6. Cook for 30-40 minutes, or until the potatoes are golden and crispy.
7. Serve and enjoy!

Nutritional Values: Calories: 230, Fat: 8g, Carbohydrates: 34g, Protein: 4g

Air Fryer Spicy Chicken Wings

Preparation time: 10 minutes
Cooking time: 20 minutes
Number of servings: 4
Ingredients:

- 1 kg chicken wings, washed and patted dry
- 2 tablespoons olive oil (30ml)
- 1 tablespoon smoked paprika
- 1 teaspoon dried oregano
- 1 teaspoon garlic powder
- 1 teaspoon cayenne pepper
- Salt and pepper to taste

Directions:
1. Preheat the air fryer to 180°C.
2. Place the chicken wings in a large bowl and drizzle with olive oil.
3. In a separate bowl, mix together the paprika, oregano, garlic powder, cayenne pepper, salt, and pepper.
4. Sprinkle the spice mixture over the chicken wings and mix until evenly coated.
5. Place the chicken wings into the air fryer basket.
6. Cook for 20 minutes, or until the wings are crunchy and done.
7. Serve and enjoy!

Nutritional Values: Calories: 451, Fat: 33g, Carbohydrates: 4g, Protein: 32g

Cheese and Bacon Puffs

Preparation time: 10 minutes
Cooking time: 15 minutes
Number of servings: 4

Ingredients:
- 1 sheet puff pastry (220g)
- 50g bacon, cooked and chopped
- 100g cheddar cheese, grated
- 1 egg, beaten

Directions:
1. Preheat the air fryer to 200°C.
2. Cut the puff pastry into 24 equal squares.
3. Place the bacon and cheese in the center of each square.

4. Fold the puff pastry over to create a triangle shape and press the edges to seal.
5. Brush the puffs with beaten egg.
6. Place the puffs into the air fryer basket.
7. Cook for 15 minutes, or until golden and crispy.
8. Serve and enjoy!

Nutritional Values: Calories: 272, Fat: 19g, Carbohydrates: 18g, Protein: 10g

Air Fryer Sausage Rolls

Preparation Time: 10 minutes
Cooking Time: 15 minutes
Number of Servings: 4

Ingredients:
- 350g sausage meat
- 2 tablespoons plain flour
- 1 large egg
- 2 sheets of puff pastry
- 1 tablespoon of vegetable oil
- Salt and pepper, to taste

Directions:
1. Preheat the air fryer to 200°C.
2. In a large bowl, mix together the sausage meat, egg and flour.
3. Season with salt and pepper.
4. Cut each sheet of puff pastry into 4 long strips.
5. Place a spoonful of the sausage meat mixture onto one end of each strip.
6. Roll up the pastry and seal the edges.

7. Brush the rolls with vegetable oil.
8. Place the rolls in the air fryer and cook for 15 minutes, turning halfway through.
9. Serve warm.

Nutritional Values: Calories: 434, Carbohydrates: 20g, Protein: 16g, Fat: 33g

Air Fryer Pigs in Blankets

Preparation Time: 10 minutes
Cooking Time: 20 minutes
Number of Servings: 4

Ingredients:
- 8 sausages
- 8 slices of bacon
- 2 tablespoons of vegetable oil
- Salt and pepper, to taste

Directions:
1. Preheat the air fryer to 180°C.
2. Cut each slice of bacon into 4 pieces.
3. Wrap each sausage with a piece of bacon and secure with a toothpick.
4. Brush the pigs in blankets with vegetable oil.
5. Place them in the air fryer and cook for 20 minutes, turning halfway through.
6. Serve warm.

Nutritional Values: Calories: 463, Carbohydrates: 2g, Protein: 19g, Fat: 40g

Air Fryer Mozzarella Sticks

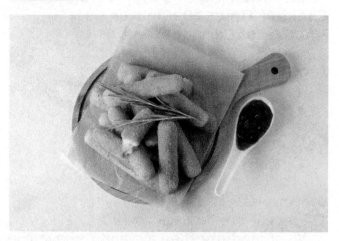

Preparation Time: 15 minutes
Cooking Time: 5 minutes
Number of Servings: 4

Ingredients:
- 8 mozzarella sticks
- 2 eggs
- 50g plain flour
- 50g breadcrumbs
- 1 teaspoon garlic powder
- 1 teaspoon onion powder
- Pinch of salt and pepper

Directions:
1. Preheat the air fryer to 180°C.
2. In a bowl, whisk together the eggs.
3. In a separate bowl, combine the flour, breadcrumbs, garlic powder, onion powder, salt, and pepper.
4. Dip each mozzarella stick in the egg mixture and then dredge in the flour mixture.
5. Place the mozzarella sticks in the preheated air fryer and cook for 5 minutes until golden brown and crispy.
6. Serve immediately.

Nutritional Values: Calories: 230, Fat: 10.2g, Carbohydrates: 21.4g, Protein: 11.1g

Air Fryer Kale Chips

Preparation Time: 10 minutes
Cooking Time: 10 minutes
Number of Servings: 4

Ingredients:
- 1 bunch of kale
- 2 tablespoons olive oil
- ½ teaspoon garlic powder
- ½ teaspoon onion powder
- Pinch of salt and pepper

Directions:
1. Preheat the air fryer to 180°C.
2. Wash and dry the kale and remove the stems.
3. Cut the kale into bite-sized pieces and place in a bowl.
4. Drizzle with olive oil and season with garlic powder, onion powder, salt, and pepper.
5. Toss the kale until it is evenly coated with the seasoning.
6. Place the kale in the preheated air fryer and cook for 10 minutes until crispy.
7. Serve immediately.

Nutritional Values: Calories: 73, Fat: 5.9g, Carbohydrates: 4.3g, Protein: 2.1g

Cheese and Jalapeno Poppers

Preparation time: 10 minutes
Cooking time: 10 minutes

Number of servings: 4

Ingredients:
- 8 jalapeno peppers, halved lengthwise and seeded
- 8 tablespoons cream cheese
- 50g of shredded Cheddar cheese

Directions:
1. Preheat the air fryer to 180°C.
2. Fill each jalapeno half with 1 tablespoon of cream cheese and sprinkle with Cheddar cheese.
3. Place the jalapeno halves in the air fryer basket and cook for 10 minutes, flipping halfway through.

Nutritional values: Calories: 104, Fat: 8.6g, Carbohydrates: 3.2g, Protein: 4.6g

Mac and Cheese Bites

Preparation time: 15 minutes
Cooking time: 10 minutes
Number of servings: 4

Ingredients:
- 250g of cooked macaroni
- 60g of grated Cheddar cheese
- 60g of breadcrumbs
- 60g of teaspoon garlic powder
- 2 tablespoons olive oil

Directions:
1. Preheat the air fryer to 180°C.
2. In a bowl, combine the macaroni, Cheddar cheese, breadcrumbs, garlic powder and olive oil.
3. Scoop 1 tablespoon of the mixture and shape into a ball.
4. Place the macaroni balls in the air fryer basket and cook for 10 minutes, flipping halfway through.

Nutritional values: Calories: 228, Fat: 12.5g, Carbohydrates: 22.2g, Protein: 8.5g

Air Fryer Beer Battered Onion Rings

Preparation time: 10 minutes
Cooking time: 10 minutes
Number of servings: 4

Ingredients:
- 1 large onion, cut into 1/4-inch slices
- 120g of all-purpose flour
- 120g of beer
- 1/2 teaspoon garlic powder
- 1/2 teaspoon paprika

Directions:
1. Preheat the air fryer to 180°C.
2. In a bowl, combine the flour, beer, garlic powder and paprika.
3. Dip the onion slices in the batter and coat evenly.
4. Place the onion slices in the air fryer basket and cook for 10 minutes, flipping halfway through.

Nutritional values: Calories: 235, Fat: 3.2g, Carbohydrates: 39.4g, Protein: 5.9g

Air Fryer Buffalo Cauliflower Bites

Preparation Time: 10 minutes
Cooking Time: 20 minutes
Number of Servings: 4

Ingredients:
- 500g cauliflower florets
- 200g all-purpose flour
- 2 eggs, beaten
- 150g Buffalo sauce
- 2 tsp garlic powder
- 2 tsp onion powder
- 2 tsp smoked paprika
- 2 tsp dried oregano
- 2 tsp dried basil
- Salt and pepper, to taste

Directions:
1. Preheat the air fryer to 200°C.
2. In a bowl, mix together the all-purpose flour, eggs, garlic powder, onion powder, smoked paprika, dried oregano, dried basil, salt, and pepper.
3. Dip the cauliflower florets in the mixture and coat them evenly.
4. Place the cauliflower florets in the air fryer basket in a single layer.
5. Cook for 15 minutes at 200°C (400°F), shaking the basket every 5 minutes.
6. Add the Buffalo sauce and cook for an additional 5 minutes.
7. Serve the Buffalo cauliflower bites hot.

Nutritional Values: Calories: 270 kcal, Carbohydrates: 30 g, Protein: 11 g, Fat: 11 g

DESSERTS

Air Fryer Apple Crumble

Preparation time: 15 minutes
Cooking time: 20 minutes
Number of servings: 6

Ingredients
- 300g Granny Smith apples, peeled and diced
- 150g plain flour
- 150g light brown sugar
- 150g rolled oats
- 150g cold butter, cubed
- 2 tsp ground cinnamon
- 1/2 tsp ground nutmeg
- Pinch of salt

Directions:
1. Preheat the air fryer to 180°C.
2. Place the diced apples in a bowl and mix with the cinnamon, nutmeg, and salt.
3. In a separate bowl, mix together the flour, sugar, and rolled oats.
4. Add the cubed butter and mix with your hands until it resembles breadcrumbs.
5. Place the apple mixture in the air fryer basket and spread the crumble mix over the top.
6. Cook for 20 minutes or until golden brown and bubbly.
7. Serve with cream or ice cream.

Nutrition values: Calories: 295, Protein: 4.2g, Fat: 12.2g, Carbohydrates: 43.4g

Air Fryer Chocolate Cake

Preparation time: 15 minutes
Cooking time: 25 minutes
Number of servings: 8

Ingredients:
- 200g dark chocolate, chopped
- 200g butter, softened
- 200g caster sugar
- 4 eggs
- 100g self-raising flour
- 2 tablespoons cocoa powder

Directions:
1. Preheat the air fryer to 160°C.
2. Place the chopped chocolate and butter in a heat-proof bowl and microwave in 30-second intervals until melted.
3. In a large bowl, beat together the caster sugar, eggs, self-raising flour and cocoa powder.
4. Gradually add in the melted chocolate mixture, stirring continuously.
5. Grease and line a 20cm springform cake tin.
6. Pour the cake mixture into the tin and place in the air fryer.
7. Cook for 25 minutes or until a skewer comes out clean.
8. Allow to cool before serving.

Nutritional values: Calories: 340, Fat: 21g, Carbohydrates: 36g, Protein: 5g

Strawberry Cheesecake

Preparation time: 15 minutes
Cooking time: 25 minutes
Number of servings: 8

Ingredients:
- 250g digestive biscuits
- 100g butter, melted
- 500g cream cheese
- 200g caster sugar
- 2 tablespoons cornflour
- 2 eggs
- 2 tablespoons lemon juice
- 200g strawberries, chopped

Directions:
1. Preheat the air fryer to 160°C.
2. Place the digestive biscuits in a food processor and process until fine crumbs.
3. Add the melted butter and process again until combined.
4. Grease and line a 20cm springform cake tin.
5. Press the biscuit mixture into the bottom of the tin and place in the air fryer.
6. Cook for 10 minutes.
7. Meanwhile, in a large bowl, beat together the cream cheese, caster sugar and cornflour until smooth.
8. Add in the eggs and lemon juice and mix until combined.
9. Stir in the chopped strawberries.
10. Pour the cheesecake mixture over the biscuit base and place back in the air fryer.
11. Cook for 15 minutes or until the cheesecake has set.
12. Allow to cool before serving.

Nutritional values: Calories: 437, Fat: 24g, Carbohydrates: 42g, Protein: 8g

Toffee Apple Crisps

Preparation time: 10 minutes
Cooking time: 10 minutes
Number of servings: 4

Ingredients:
- 2 large apples, peeled and thinly sliced
- 2 tablespoons caster sugar
- 2 tablespoons toffee sauce

Directions:
1. Preheat the air fryer to 180°C.
2. Place the apple slices in a bowl and sprinkle over the caster sugar.
3. Toss until the apples are well coated.
4. Place the apple slices in the air fryer and cook for 10 minutes or until golden brown and crispy.
5. Drizzle over the toffee sauce.
6. Serve immediately.

Nutritional values: Calories: 128, Fat: 2g, Carbohydrates: 28g, Protein: 0.4g

Air Fryer Coconut Ice Cream

Preparation time: 10 minutes
Cooking time: 15 minutes
Number of servings: 4

Ingredients:
- 400 g coconut cream
- 50 g caster sugar
- 50 g desiccated coconut

Directions:
1. In a medium bowl, combine the coconut cream and caster sugar and mix until combined.
2. Place the coconut cream mixture in the air fryer basket.
3. Set the air fryer to 180°C and cook for 15 minutes.
4. Once cooked, allow to cool slightly before stirring in the desiccated coconut.
5. Serve immediately in your favourite ice cream dishes.

Nutritional values: Calories: 474, Fat: 39.9 g, Carbohydrates: 28.2 g, Protein: 4.2 g

Air Fryer Doughnuts

Preparation time: 15 minutes
Cooking time: 8 minutes
Number of servings: 10

Ingredients:
- 400g of plain flour
- 1/4 teaspoon baking soda
- 1/4 teaspoon baking powder
- 1/2 teaspoon ground cinnamon
- 1/4 teaspoon ground nutmeg
- 150g of light brown sugar
- 180 ml of buttermilk
- 1 large egg
- 3 tablespoons (45 g) butter, melted
- 1 teaspoon vanilla extract

Directions:

1. In a large bowl, combine the flour, baking soda, baking powder, cinnamon, nutmeg, and brown sugar and mix until combined.
2. In a separate bowl, combine the buttermilk, egg, melted butter, and vanilla extract and mix until combined.
3. Add the wet ingredients to the dry ingredients and mix until a dough forms.
4. Place the dough in the air fryer basket and flatten to the desired shape.
5. Set the air fryer to 200°C and cook for 8 minutes.
6. Once cooked, remove from the air fryer and allow to cool before serving.

Nutritional values: Calories: 293, Fat: 10.3 g, Carbohydrates: 43.5 g, Protein: 5.2 g

Air Fryer Banoffee Pie

Preparation time: 15 minutes
Cooking time: 10 minutes
Number of servings: 8

Ingredients:
- 80g of butter
- 80g of light brown sugar
- 1 (400 g) can condensed milk
- 1/2 teaspoon ground cinnamon
- 1/2 teaspoon ground nutmeg
- 1/2 teaspoon ground ginger
- 1/4 teaspoon ground cloves
- 1/2 teaspoon salt

- 1 (250 g) packet digestive biscuits
- 2 (400 g) cans banana slices
- 2 tablespoons (30 g) cocoa powder

Directions:
1. In a medium saucepan, melt the butter and add the brown sugar, condensed milk, cinnamon, nutmeg, ginger, cloves, and salt.
2. Cook the mixture over low heat, stirring continuously, until it begins to thicken.
3. Place the digestive biscuits in the air fryer basket and cook for 7 minutes at 180°C.
4. Once the biscuits are cooked, remove from the air fryer and place in a large bowl.
5. Add the cooked butter and sugar mixture to the bowl and mix until everything is combined.
6. Grease a 20cm pie dish with butter and pour the mixture into the dish.
7. Arrange the banana slices over the mixture, sprinkle with cocoa powder, and place in the air fryer.
8. Cook for 3 minutes at 180°C.
9. Once cooked, allow to cool before serving.

Nutritional values: Calories: 538, Fat: 20.3 g, Carbohydrates: 77.4 g, Protein: 9.4 g

Air Fryer Brownies

Preparation time: 15 minutes
Cooking time: 10 minutes
Number of servings: 8

Ingredients:
- 100g of butter
- 100g of dark chocolate
- 100g of caster sugar
- 2 large eggs
- 1 teaspoon vanilla extract
- 120g of plain flour
- 1/4 teaspoon baking powder
- 1/4 teaspoon baking soda

Directions:
1. In a medium saucepan, melt the butter and dark chocolate over low heat.
2. Once melted, remove from the heat and add the caster sugar. Stir until combined.
3. Add the eggs and vanilla extract and mix until combined.
4. In a separate bowl, combine the flour, baking powder, and baking soda and mix until combined.
5. Add the dry ingredients to the wet ingredients and mix until a thick batter forms.
6. Grease a 22cm cake tin with butter and pour the batter into the tin.
7. Place the tin in the air fryer and cook for 10 minutes at 180°C.
8. Once cooked, remove from the air fryer and allow to cool before serving.

Nutritional values: Calories: 298, Fat: 18.3 g, Carbohydrates: 31.3 g, Protein: 3.6 g

Air Fryer Lemon Meringue Pie

Preparation time: 20 minutes
Cooking time: 15 minutes
Number of servings: 8

Ingredients:
- Shortcrust pastry, 320g
- Caster sugar, 120g

- Cornflour, 30g
- Lemon juice, 200ml
- Egg yolks, 3
- Unsalted butter, 30g
- Meringue, 200g

Directions:
1. Roll out the pastry and line a 20cm pie dish.
2. Preheat the air fryer to 180°C.
3. In a bowl, mix together the caster sugar, cornflour, lemon juice and egg yolks.
4. Pour the mix into the pastry case and dot with butter.
5. Put the pie into the air fryer and cook for 12 minutes.
6. Remove the pie from the air fryer, top with meringue and cook for 3 minutes.

Nutritional values: Calories: 270, Carbohydrates: 37g, Fats: 13g, Proteins: 4g

Air Fryer Rhubarb Crumble

Preparation time: 20 minutes
Cooking time: 15 minutes
Number of servings: 4

Ingredients:
- 400 g Rhubarb
- 50 g Light brown sugar
- 100 g Unsalted butter
- 100 g Plain flour
- 1 teaspoon Ground cinnamon
- ½ teaspoon Ground ginger

Directions:
1. Preheat the air fryer to 180°C.
2. In a bowl, combine the rhubarb, light brown sugar, butter, plain flour, ground cinnamon and ginger.
3. Spoon the mix into a greased baking dish.
4. Place the dish into the air fryer and cook for 12 minutes.

5. Remove the dish from the air fryer and let cool for a few minutes.

Nutritional values: Calories: 204, Carbohydrates: 24g, Fats: 11g, Proteins: 2g

Air Fryer Sticky Toffee Pudding

Preparation time: 25 minutes
Cooking time: 15 minutes
Number of servings: 6

Ingredients:
- 200 g Dates
- 250 ml Boiling water
- 1 teaspoon Bicarbonate of soda
- 100 g Self-raising flour
- 70 g Unsalted butter
- 70 g Dark brown sugar
- 2 Eggs
- 1 teaspoon Vanilla extract
- Toffee sauce, to serve

Directions:
1. Preheat the air fryer to 180°C.
2. Put the dates in a bowl and pour over the boiling water.
3. Add the bicarbonate of soda and leave to one side.
4. In a separate bowl, cream together the butter and sugar.
5. Beat in the eggs and the vanilla extract.

6. Add the flour, dates and the remaining liquid.
7. Pour the mix into a greased ovenproof dish.
8. Place the dish into the air fryer basket and cook for 15 minutes.
9. Remove from the air fryer and serve with toffee sauce.

Nutritional values: Calories: 255, Carbohydrates: 35g, Fats: 11g, Proteins: 4g

Air Fryer Peach Cobbler

Preparation time: 15 minutes
Cooking time: 20 minutes
Number of servings: 6

Ingredients:
• 150g all-purpose flour
• 4 teaspoons baking powder
• 70g brown sugar
• 1/2 teaspoon salt
• 120ml whole milk
• 1 teaspoon vanilla extract
• 70g butter, melted
• 2 large peaches, peeled and sliced
• 2 tablespoons sugar

Directions:
1. Preheat the air fryer to 180°C.
2. In a large bowl, combine the flour, baking powder, brown sugar and salt.
3. In a separate bowl, whisk together the milk, vanilla extract and melted butter.
4. Add the wet ingredients to the dry ingredients and mix until combined.
5. Grease the air fryer basket with cooking spray.
6. Spread the batter into the basket and top with the peach slices. Sprinkle with sugar.
7. Place the basket in the air fryer and cook for 20 minutes.
8. Serve warm with a dollop of cream or ice cream.

Nutritional Values: Calories: 226, Fat: 8.3g, Carbohydrates: 33.3g, Protein: 4.1g

Air Fryer Bread Pudding

Preparation time: 15 minutes
Cooking time: 25 minutes
Number of servings: 6

Ingredients:
• 300g stale bread, cubed
• 2 eggs
• 300ml whole milk
• 25g sugar
• 1/2 teaspoon ground cinnamon
• 1/4 teaspoon ground nutmeg
• 75g raisins
• 2 tablespoons butter, melted

Directions:
1. Preheat the air fryer to 180°C.
2. In a large bowl, whisk together the eggs, milk, sugar, cinnamon and nutmeg.
3. Add the bread cubes and raisins and mix until combined.
4. Grease the air fryer basket with cooking spray.
5. Pour the bread pudding mixture into the basket and drizzle with melted butter.
6. Place the basket in the air fryer and cook for 25 minutes.
7. Serve warm with a dollop of cream or ice cream.

Nutritional Values: Calories: 252, Fat: 8.1g, Carbohydrates: 35.9g, Protein: 7.8g

Air Fryer Eton Mess

Preparation time: 10 minutes
Cooking time: 15 minutes
Number of servings: 6

Ingredients:
- 6 meringue nests
- 300g fresh strawberries, hulled and halved
- 300ml whipped cream
- 25g icing sugar

Directions:
1. Preheat the air fryer to 180°C.
2. Grease the air fryer basket with cooking spray.
3. Place the meringue nests in the basket and cook for 15 minutes.
4. Meanwhile, in a large bowl, combine the strawberries, whipped cream and icing sugar.
5. When the meringue nests are done cooking, break them up and add them to the strawberry mixture.
6. Serve the Eton Mess immediately.

Nutritional Values: Calories: 234, Fat: 10.8g, Carbohydrates: 30.6g, Protein: 3.6g

Air Fryer Chocolate Chip Cookies

Preparation time 15 minutes
Cooking time: 15 minutes
Number of servings: 12

Ingredients:
- 150g all-purpose flour
- 1 teaspoon baking powder
- 1/2 teaspoon salt
- 100g butter, softened
- 50g light brown sugar
- 50g granulated sugar
- 1 egg
- 1 teaspoon vanilla extract
- 150g semi-sweet chocolate chips

Directions:
1. Preheat the air fryer to 180°C.
2. In a large bowl, combine the flour, baking powder and salt.
3. In a separate bowl, cream together the butter, brown sugar and granulated sugar until light and fluffy.
4. Beat in the egg and vanilla extract.
5. Gradually add the dry ingredients to the wet ingredients, mixing until combined.
6. Stir in the chocolate chips.
7. Grease the air fryer basket with cooking spray.
8. Divide the cookie dough into 12 equal portions and place them in the basket.
9. Place the basket in the air fryer and cook for 15 minutes.
10. Serve warm with a glass of milk.

Nutritional Values: Calories: 214, Fat: 11.5g, Carbohydrates: 25.5g, Protein: 2.8g

Caramel Popcorn

Preparation time: 10 minutes
Cooking time: 10 minutes
Number of Servings: 4

Ingredients:
- 100g popcorn kernels
- 50g butter
- 100g brown sugar
- 2 tablespoons of golden syrup

Directions:
1. Preheat the air fryer to 160 °C.
2. Place the popcorn kernels in the air fryer and cook for 10 minutes.
3. Place the butter, sugar, and syrup in a small saucepan over medium heat and stir until the butter has melted and the mixture is bubbling.
4. Pour the caramel mixture over the cooked popcorn, stirring to coat.
5. Place the popcorn back into the air fryer and cook for an additional 5 minutes.

Nutritional values: Calories: 300, Fat: 12g, Carbohydrates: 44g, Protein: 2.7g

Air Fryer Chocolate Fondant

Preparation time: 10 minutes
Cooking time: 15 minutes
Number of servings: 4

Ingredients:
- 120g plain flour
- 90g caster sugar
- 50g cocoa powder
- 2 eggs
- 150g butter, melted
- 150g dark chocolate, melted
- 2 tablespoons of milk

Directions:
1. In a medium bowl, sift together the plain flour, caster sugar, and cocoa powder.
2. In a separate bowl, whisk together the eggs and melted butter.
3. Slowly pour the egg and butter mixture into the dry ingredients and mix until combined.
4. Add in the melted dark chocolate and milk and mix together until smooth.
5. Grease 4 ramekins with butter and pour the mixture into them.
6. Place the ramekins in the air fryer and cook for 15 minutes at 180°C.
7. Serve with a dollop of cream or ice cream.

Nutritional Values: Calories: 493, Protein: 6.3g, Carbohydrates: 31.1g, Fats: 36.5g

Air Fryer Eccles Cake

Preparation time: 15 minutes
Cooking time: 20 minutes
Number of servings: 8

Ingredients:
- 250g plain flour
- 1 teaspoon baking powder
- 120g butter
- 100g caster sugar
- 2 tablespoons of golden syrup
- 2 tablespoons of currants
- 2 tablespoons of sultanas
- 2 tablespoons of mixed peel
- 1 teaspoon of ground cinnamon
- 1 egg, beaten
- 1 tablespoon of milk

Directions:
1. In a medium bowl, sift together the plain flour and baking powder.
2. Add the butter and rub together with your fingertips until the mixture looks like fine breadcrumbs.
3. Stir in the caster sugar, golden syrup, currants, sultanas, mixed peel, and ground cinnamon.
4. Mix in the beaten egg and milk until the mixture forms a dough.
5. Roll the dough out to a thickness of 1cm and cut into 8 circles.
6. Place the circles into the air fryer and cook for 20 minutes at 160°C.
7. Serve warm with a dollop of cream or ice cream.

Nutritional Values: Calories: 282, Protein: 3.3g, Carbohydrates: 32.6g, Fats: 15.3g

Air Fryer Bananas Foster

Preparation time: 10 minutes
Cooking time: 10 minutes
Number of servings: 4

Ingredients:
- 4 bananas, sliced into thick rounds
- 2 tablespoons of butter
- 2 tablespoons of light brown sugar
- 2 tablespoons of dark rum
- 2 tablespoons of toasted almond flakes
- 2 tablespoons of honey
- 2 teaspoons of ground cinnamon

Directions:
1. Place the sliced bananas in the air fryer and cook for 10 minutes at 160°C.
2. In a small saucepan, melt the butter and add the light brown sugar and dark rum.
3. Bring the mixture to the boil and remove from the heat.
4. Add the toasted almond flakes, honey, and ground cinnamon to the saucepan and stir together.
5. Place the cooked bananas in the saucepan and stir together until the bananas are coated with the sauce.
6. Serve the Bananas Foster with a dollop of cream or ice cream.

Nutritional Values: Calories: 229, Protein: 1.7g, Carbohydrates: 24.4g, Fats: 12.2g

Printed in Great Britain
by Amazon

23409246R00044